ADVANCE PRAISE

"As the CEO of a billion dollar company that engages hundreds of thousands of entrepreneurial sales leaders around the world, I couldn't think of a better book than *Lessons from Great Lives* from which to learn and be motivated. Sill was a shining star in the world of leadership development long before self- absorbed gurus cashed in on clever formulas and catch phrases. "

—Truman Hunt
CEO, Nu Skin Enterprises, Inc. (NYSE:NUS)
Chairman, World Federation of Direct Selling Associations

"As a student of history and success, this may be as significant a read as I could recommend. I cannot think of a better course of study for improving our lives than to study some of the greatest minds that ever lived. "

—Richard Paul Evans
New York Times #1 best selling author
and founder of Bookwise

"If you want to transform your life, don't just read this book. . . study it. It will help you to become the unstoppable person you want to be."

—Cynthia Kersey
Author of the best-selling books,
Unstoppable & Unstoppable Women

"We live in a world where the meaning of the word "rich" has been badly polluted. What a breath of fresh air this book can bring to our lives; hard work and character count! It's a must read for anyone who wants to be truly wealthy!"

—Dave Blanchard
CEO, Og Mandino Group

"I have worked with Dan McCormick for years and know him to be one of the most inspiring, well read and knowledgeable people in our industry. I hope that many of the 500,000 distributors I have worldwide will read and study this book. Reading about these great lives can truly transform yours."

—Nathan Ricks
Team Elite, Nu Skin Enterprises

"Dan McCormick has discovered a hidden treasure and is sharing it with all of us. If you want to be the best at anything in life, open the pages and you'll find inspiration to train your mind. This book is more valuable than gold!"

—Peter Vidmar
Nationally acclaimed speaker and author
Olympic Gold Medalist

"I loved it! Dan McCormick has unearthed a brilliant book

from the past. A must read for all those that want to be rich in every area of their life. I use it constantly as a reference for ideas, wisdom and inspiration. "

—Kevin Hall
Author of *The Power of Words for Leaders*

"What a treasure! A book inspired by the original Hall of Fame in America. Some of the greatest minds reside here for your inspiration. Some of the greatest lives ever lived are in this book for your reward. Dan McCormick has brought a new heightened level of awareness back to foundational teachings that shaped our country and can change your life! "

—Art and Susan Zuckerman
Directors, Hall of Fame for Great Americans

"Powerful! Dan has successfully captured the wisdom of the ages. This book contains the greatest thinkers, leaders, and achievers of all time. If you want success, then study and apply the principles in this book. "

—TJ Hoisington
Bestselling author of *If You Think You Can!*

"Twenty-one years ago, Dan McCormick challenged me to read the third book of my life at forty years of age! Since that time, my wife Sue, and I, have earned over 15 million dollars. If Dan is recommending another book to you, I would certainly listen; it could change your life. "

—Bob Burdick
NSA National Marketing Director

LESSONS FROM
GREAT
LIVES

LEARN TO BE RICH IN
ALL AREAS OF YOUR LIFE!

STERLING W. SILL
& DAN McCORMICK

Co-authored by Kristina Booth

AYLESBURY
PUBLISHING

ISBN 0-9776288-0-9

First Edition
10 9 8 7 6 5 4 3 2 1

CONTENTS

WE NEED TO KNOW THE JOY OF BEING ALIVE, THE JOYS OF EXCELLENCE, AND THE JOYS OF TRUTH. WE NEED TO KNOW THE JOYS OF LABOR, THE JOYS OF FAMILY, AND THE JOYS OF BEING GENUINE. IT IS WONDERFUL TO MAKE A PROFIT. IT IS GREAT TO DEVELOP PROMINENCE AND IT IS STIMULATING TO ACQUIRE FAME, BUT EVEN GLORY HAS NO HALO IF WE MISS THE JOY. DURING MY MANY YEARS, I HAVE LOVED LIFE, I HAVE BEEN BROADENED BY THE LAW, I HAVE BEEN INSPIRED BY LOVE, I HAVE BEEN THRILLED BY SUCCESS, AND I HAVE GLORIED IN STRUGGLE AND HARDSHIP, BUT I THANK THE GREAT GOD OF THE UNIVERSE THAT I HAVE NOT MISSED THE JOY.

STERLING W. SILL
1903-1994

PREFACE

Literature is a window to mankind's social evolution. By studying various forms of literature over the ages, we can determine with a fair amount of certainty what types of problems people faced and how they went about solving them. Across the vast expanse of time, since man began seeking a better way of life, the term "success" has been redefined with each new generation. Now, more than ever before, the marketplace is flooded with self-promoting books and seminars aimed at infusing an intense desire for the best luxuries life has to offer. Magic tricks to make our dreams materialize are revealed, and with enough practice, anyone can be a performer.

A revolution of thought has taken place in success literature. We have abandoned the deeply rooted principles of hard work, ingenuity, and focused study, to embrace the hot new trends of the "go-go" 90's followed by the technological wizardry of the "roaring" 2000's. Left behind in this march towards the ultimate reward of complete fulfillment, were teachings based on universal laws that encompassed ethics, values, character, honest labor, and foundational truths. As a result, our brains have been sautéed in a desire for urgent riches at all costs. Massive fortunes have been made in real estate, stock valuations, energy, oil, precious metals, and various entrepreneurial endeavors. Because of this, it now appears that countless individuals are experts on creating wealth. Many ignore traditional values as they seek to push us towards the self aggrandizing promotion of "Me."

Dazzling covers adorn the shelves of book stores flaunting big houses, fancy sports cars, lavish lifestyles, and often times, crude titles to grab your attention. Promises are given such as, "Follow me, learn my secrets, and you can achieve total financial freedom in twenty minutes a day." Or, "Give us one hour and we will have you on your way to financial independence..." blah, blah, blah. The modern day writer of success literature is often times a self-proclaimed guru who suffers from a fatty enlargement of the ego! Have YOU gotten rich from their advice? Have your friends become wildly successful in their pursuits by learning the "system" to achieving great wealth found in these books? Most would agree that this is not the case.

Instead, many people have become frustrated or disheartened, savings accounts have been depleted, relationships have been ruined, and worst of all, faith in one's own abilities has been fractured. It is time to reground ourselves in teachings of the purest form. Such teachings have been proven over and over again, throughout history, to build character, to develop life skills, to instill courage, and to strengthen resolve to reach for and obtain that which will bring us true happiness.

Lessons from Great Lives will transport you back in

time to meet people of extraordinary strength, ingenuity, and self mastery. The lives that were selected for our study were not driven by the pursuit of riches or of fame. Instead, they lived lives of hard work, of diligence, and of concentration on principles that propelled them forward in their worthy pursuits. The power and greatness in these men and women provide an inexhaustible source of time-tested wisdom that can produce results, results that can make you rich in all areas of your life.

It has been said that a chemist, a lawyer, or an inventor does not depend upon his own discoveries for his occupational success. Instead, he appropriates for his use all the tested methods and proven formulas of the best men in his field. If utilizing the most helpful past experiences of others is a necessity for business or professional success, why shouldn't the lessons of great men and women be used just as profitably in the larger and more important field of life itself?

This book, which you now hold in your hand, has motivated me to take more action in my life than any other form of personal progress instruction. As I speak to thousands of people each year, yearning for direction, for instruction on how to achieve their dreams, I am repeatedly asked, "Are there any books you recommend that will teach me what you have learned to become so successful?"

During the journey of my life, I have enjoyed the writings of countless authors on the subject of personal development and empowerment including literature from centuries ago to the present. None have influenced me in such a profound way as did my first reading of Sterling W. Sill's masterpiece, *Lessons from Great Lives*, published in 1981. As if the oracles of human development were seated beside me, I absorbed their wisdom with gratitude for the lives they lived, for the lessons they learned, and for the courage they portrayed. If I took only a small portion of the universal laws they had unfolded and applied them in my life, I could achieve my dreams. Their lessons were for me and they are for you as well.

Sterling W. Sill was a prolific and accomplished author, dynamic leader, popular speaker, and devoted student of philosophy whose career spanned more than forty years. He authored over thirty books, delivered countless inspirational speeches, and hosted a radio program that touched the lives of millions. It was his mission to teach the majesty of the human mind as a great workshop where ordinary people can be reborn into the greatness for which they were intended.

You have, in your hand, one of Sill's masterpieces, lost to the masses for the last twenty-five years, having been pushed aside by publications that promised a magic formula of instant success. After visiting the famous Hall of Fame for Great Americans in New York City, where the lives of American heroes are honored, I became acutely aware of the need for guiding lights that illuminate our path to the richness we all seek. It was time, I felt, to dust off the cover of the book that steered me in the direction of constant progress towards my goals.

Short cuts to success are all around us, yet few seem to get there quicker or even arrive at their chosen destination. By republishing *Lessons from Great Lives*, and providing this wealth of time tested wisdom to the masses once again, I believe that ordinary men and women can become extraordinary. It has been said that a tree can only grow so tall, but a man has no limits. Dreams can become realities, whether it is to prosper in relationships, in business, in material wealth, or in spiritual paths. Learn the lessons found in this book, apply the wisdom, and experience the metamorphosis that is mankind's greatest achievement . . . happiness.

Someone once asked a famous writer, "When were you born?" and he replied, "I will tell you about it. It was one Sunday afternoon about 3:30 just after I had finished reading a great book." It is my sincerest hope that this book will be a new beginning of richness in your life.

You are the heir to wisdom that has already been discovered, has already been tested, and has already been proven. In an unwavering commitment to truth and the pursuit of it, the brilliant philosopher, Socrates, seized upon the idea that the great minds that had gone before him, and also those who were currently studying the mysteries of the world, were a valuable resource to maximize his efforts. He had only one lifetime to discover truth and to enjoy the fruits of happiness that it would bring. Thus, he gave this counsel, "Employ your time in improving yourself by other men's writings, so that you gain easily what others have labored hard for."

It is with great humility that I present to you a portrait of nineteen people who applied tremendous diligence, focus, and concentration on implementing universal and time honored principles of success in their lives. May the results of their persistent efforts illuminate your path and guide you towards richness in life that is everlasting.

Enjoy the journey,
Dan McCormick

YOUR
HALL OF
FAME

I n 1899, a substantial monetary gift made to New York University was used under the direction of Chancellor Henry M. McCracken to erect an awe inspiring memorial to success called, The Hall of Fame for Great Americans. Located on a beautiful site in Bronx, New York, it was designed as a circular terrace in form, with a superimposed open- air colonnade connecting the University's Hall of Philosophy with the Hall of Languages. Membership in this Hall of Fame was limited to those who had been dead for at least twenty- five years and who received a majority vote of the one- hundred prominent Americans who made up the electoral college. Only one- hundred and two great Americans have been selected for membership since 1900 and each of these is represented in the Hall of Fame by a bronze bust and commemorative tablet. This historical institution represents the most outstanding gathering of greatness in the world and is evidenced by the finest collection of statuary.

Centuries ago, the ancient Greeks gave a little different

twist to this Hall of Fame idea by putting it on a much grander scale. They chose Mt. Olympus, whose summit reaches some 10,000 feet, as the home for their great mythological heroes and national deities. Around these Olympian personalities, the Greeks composed literature picturing the strength and describing the virtues of these super mortals who, in their imaginations, inhabited this sacred mountain top. Poems, songs, and stories were written on a heroic scale to match the magnificence of the mountain upon which they lived.

The heroic is defined as something that is larger than life. When we look up to those having heroic ideals and ambitions, we tend to mold our minds and hearts to heroic aspirations and tend to perform heroic deeds. During this golden age, Greek culture reached a height that, in many ways, has never been surpassed. The influence from the top of Mt. Olympus was an important factor in drawing the Greeks up to their high place among the nations of that day. What else but greatness could be expected from the people of Sparta who believed themselves to be descendants of Hercules? They talked about his feats, they breathed his courage, and they relived his greatness. As a consequence, they became natural heirs to his strength.

Regardless of the size of the body, ambitions can also be formed in a giant mold. Minds can be broadened, hearts can be enlarged, and spirits can be given greater power. One cannot long remain small while he is thinking and living big. Greatness can be made to reproduce itself in the lives of others.

There are several outstanding opportunities in every individual life where some adaptation to this hall of fame idea can be used to great advantage. Each of us may have our own

Mt. Olympus, constructed with heroes of our own selection. We need someone to look up to, someone to admire, someone to love, and someone with whom we can feel a close kinship. We need more actual working models of righteous accomplishment formed to heroic specifications.

In his book, *Heroes and Hero Worship*, Thomas Carlyle said, "Great men taken up in any way are very profitable company, for we cannot so much as look upon a great man without gaining something from him." We cannot entertain in our minds and hearts the great patriots, or the great scientists, or the great religious leaders, without bringing ourselves to resemble them more intimately. As the flower reaches up toward the light of the sun, so every human being has an instinctive tendency to reach up to those who embody traits more noble than his own. Carlyle refers to this procedure of reaching upward as heroism, or hero worship. It is a tendency where we can make one man great by the inspiration of other great men.

Carlyle describes worship as "admiration without limit or limitation." Whatever this relationship may be called, or whatever its degree of intensity, there is a powerful attraction involved that may be used for our own uplift and benefit. This idea is very closely related to the two great Christian religious commandments. When we reach up to God with all our hearts, we will then love our neighbors as ourselves. By doing this, we tend to make virtues, great and small, our own.

We may have a kind of private hall of fame of our own choosing, or develop an individual Mt. Olympus reserved exclusively for those great men and women who can most profitably influence the direction and extent of our lives. Those we would admit to this private sanctuary would be the ones who are most able to set our hearts afire with devotion for truth. They could serve us as an example as they personify faith and make fidelity real for us. They would repulse what is unclean or unfair, and strike a direct blow at the painted faces of falsehood and deceit.

A person who provides a good example has the blessed ability of arousing a desire in others to develop their own talents and aptitudes to their upper limits. The tremendous upward pull that one personality may have upon another might be compared to the attraction that the planets exert as they hold each other in their orbits. Such was the case with Socrates who projected a strong positive influence upon the life of Plato. We know of the personal benefit that Jesus bestowed upon Simon Peter, and the power by which Beatrice inspired Dante. We also know that Nancy Hanks had an indelible influence upon her son, Abraham Lincoln. A more current example is the relationship between the famous golfer, Tiger Woods, and his father whom Tiger credits for influencing every aspect of his greatness.

Before the people whom we hold up as an ideal can exert their maximum power, we must get ourselves within their magnetic range. Try to imagine how much Carl Sandburg added to his own life by becoming the admirer and biographer of Abraham Lincoln. Great men become more powerful in our lives as our knowledge and love of them increases. When we know Lincoln as well as Sandburg knew him, we can profit from that relationship. Greatness feeds upon itself, and men can absorb other men.

There is an interesting account in the Old Testament that explains how young King Saul qualified as King of Israel. The record says, ". . . and there went with (Saul) a band of

4

men, whose hearts God had touched. " (I Sam. 10:26) That is, Saul had his own hall of fame. James Preston Burke wrote a stimulating poem based on this beautiful passage of scripture which he entitled, *"Bands of Men."*

> Lord, don't send us out to battle alone
> Amid the entanglements of life's unknown,
> But support and cheer us, thou guardian friend,
> In bonds of fellowship with bands of men.
> Much is perplexing in life's every day
> With great complications obscuring the way,
> Because we are anxious to reach the end,
> Accompany us, Lord, with bands of men.
>
> Men with compassion, men with zeal,
> Men who can think, men who can feel,
> Men whose hearts are touched by thee,
> Noble men, strong men, men who are free.

Men are judged by the company they keep. We have unlimited freedom in selecting the members of our own hall of fame, and so we might apply the same selection procedure used by an art collector when he wanted to buy an oil painting for the inner sanctum of his home. If, after viewing many paintings, he was attracted to a particular piece of art, he sat down before it and studied it thoroughly. With his most careful thoughts, he tried to fully understand its message and meaning. Then, after a lapse of a few days, he went back and looked at it again to determine whether his feeling for the picture had diminished or increased in power. After a few visits with the painting, he tried to forget it. If it was easy to forget,

5

the relationship was ended, but if the picture had grown in his mind to a point where he felt that he could not get along without it, then he bought the painting. If it had assumed an importance to him that he could not forget, then he knew that the picture would continue to grow in his mind, and that his heart would be eternally delighted and uplifted by it.

Abraham Lincoln was unique. There never has been and never will be, another man just like him. But, for that matter, every man and every woman in the world is unique. Creation makes no duplicates, and no one can ever be replaced. It would be interesting to try to imagine what it would mean to Americans if, by some unfortunate event, the memory of Abraham Lincoln was completely erased from our minds and literature. Just suppose that the unwavering honesty, the stimulating humility, the love of freedom that was represented in his life was totally expunged from our memories as though it had never existed. Then imagine the same thing happening to our memory of George Washington, Benjamin Franklin, and the ninety- nine other great Americans making up the Hall of Fame membership. What a void, what lonesomeness, and what a sense of lessening we would feel. We should be more fervently grateful for these great men and women, especially when we think what our lives might have been like if we were brought up at the feet of such men as Karl Marx, Joseph Stalin, Adolph Hitler, or Osama bin Laden.

On one pedestal in my own private hall of fame, I have placed my high school principal who served my early hero- worshipping needs. Next to him is my favorite Sunday school teacher, along with one of the most outstanding people who helped give my religious life its direction. The man who helped mold my business life also holds a prominent place.

6

Abraham Lincoln occupies a place of honor in my gallery of great men. With him are Socrates, Emerson, Moses, Gandhi, and Stradivari. I have also included Booker T. Washington, George Washington Carver, Madame Curie, and Joan of Arc. My own mother and father are prominently positioned in my inner council of great lives.

The chief place in my personal hall of fame, which is a little apart from the others, is occupied by the greatest life that ever lived, the Master of all men, the Savior and Redeemer of the world, Jesus of Nazareth. His was the only life ever lived where a mistake did not need to be made in order to discover that it was wrong. I have searched the scriptures and I have studied the individual lives of great men and women selected for my gallery. I have written up a tablet for each on which is described those qualities that I want to stamp more indelibly into my mind. Each of the one-hundred and two people in the Hall of Fame for Great Americans was selected for a particular purpose. Each of those making up my gallery was chosen because of some unique ability they possess which can help me. That is, my father serves a different place than does Abraham Lincoln, but each is indispensable in his sphere, and neither of them can ever be replaced. To each of these special advisors has been attributed a particular part of the responsibility for my success.

In my imagination, I like to go into my private hall of fame to draw strength and satisfaction from my own band of men "whose hearts God has touched." I receive a power in my soul from the wonderful gifts that God bestowed upon them, as each was so willing to spend their strength to lift me upward. Through this hall of fame philosophy, we may receive a maximum of enrichment from those wonderful gifts that God has lavished upon His gifted children. Thus we may fulfill the grateful prayer of Harry Kemp wherein he said:

> Chief of all thy wondrous works, O God
> Supreme of all thy plan.
> Thou hast put an upward reach
> Into the heart of man.

THIS IS
THE BEST
OF ME

As a kind of text for this collection of brief biographies, I would like to present an idea from Charles Dickens' *A Tale of Two Cities*. Authorship is the process by which we discover the great qualities of nations, as well as those of men and women. Certainly, one of the finest authors of our world was Charles Dickens, who was born February 7, 1812. Even to this date, in our world filled as it is with the miracles and wonders of our knowledge explosions, he is still regarded by many as the greatest English novelist of all time.

Mr. Dickens wrote sixteen great novels, including such famous master pieces as *Pickwick Papers*, *Oliver Twist*, *David Copperfield*, *A Christmas Carol*, *Great Expectations*, and *A Tale of Two Cities*. He possessed a general abundance of creative energy. He was a sheer genius as a story teller and had an exuberant style that swept his readers along in a wonderful journey of delight. It is thought by a great many that Dickens' *Christmas Carol* is the most famous non-scriptural Christmas story in the world and perhaps the best-known short story in the entire English language.

However, Dickens himself said that of all his many famous works, he liked his *A Tale of Two Cities* best. As I recently re- read some of the great events that took place preceding and following the period of The French Revolution, I thought of the many lessons that could be learned from these two great cities and the contributions made to us by the people and conditions described in this historic masterpiece.

Dickens began his account by describing some conditions preceding The French Revolution very similar to those that exist in our day. He said:

It was the best of times, it was the worst of times,
It was the age of wisdom, it was the age of foolishness,
It was the epoch of belief, it was the epoch of incredulity,
It was the season of Light, it was the season of Darkness,
It was the spring of hope, it was the winter of despair,
We had everything before us, we had nothing before us,
We were all going direct to Heaven, we were all going direct the other way.

When we experience a period of great progress or development, we often have some serious problems arise to hold the balance even. That is, it may not seem quite fair to attribute all of the good experiences to the earth in one age and all of the evil in another.

The two cities involved in the title are Paris and London. However, Mr. Dickens' great story is not so much a matter of telling about two cities, as it is in describing the lives of some important people who lived in them. Dr. Alexandre Manette, a French physician, was called in to attend a young peasant and his sister under circumstances that made him aware that the girl had been brutally mistreated and the boy mortally wounded by the Marquis de St. Evremonde and his brother, who were members of the French nobility. To prevent these members of the aristocracy from possible embarrassment, Dr. Manette was buried in the darkness of the French Bastille for eighteen years in order to guarantee his silence. During those long years in his miserable prison dungeon, Dr. Manette had become mentally deranged. Finally his release was brought about, and he was taken to England where he gradually recovered his sanity.

Charles Darnay, who concealed under that name the fact that he was a nephew of the Marquis, left France and renounced his French heritage because of his detestation of the cruel practices of the old French aristocracy. He fell in love with Lucie, Dr. Manette's daughter, and they were happily married. In the course of events, their first child was born.

During the Reign of Terror that accompanied the revolution, Darnay went back to Paris to try to save a faithful former servant who had been falsely accused of having served the selfish groups of the nobility. Upon arrival in Paris, he was himself arrested, condemned to death. He was saved at the last moment by Sydney Carton, a reckless wastrel and English barrister, whose errors in character were partially redeemed by his generous devotion to Lucie, her badly mistreated father, her husband and family. Carton, who strongly resembled Darnay in appearance, smuggled the latter out of prison and took his place for the ride to the guillotine.

On the way, Carton's real identity was discovered by a poor seamstress who had also been unjustly condemned to die. She knew that Carton was giving his life that Darnay might live and provide for his family, the members of which Carton also loved. She wanted to know why. Thrilled by his bravery, the girl said to him, ". . . will you let me hold your hand? I am not afraid, but I am little and weak, and it will give me more courage . . . O you will let me hold your brave hand?"

As they were being hauled to the execution, Sydney Carton received great satisfaction from his service as he gave his life for the woman he loved, her husband, father, and her children. Even as his death approached, it gave him a feeling of value and worthiness that in his own present excellence he had risen far above the level of his previous average.

By his prophetic thoughts, Carton projected in his mind the favorable results of his good deed by saying, "I see the lives for which I lay down my life, peaceful, useful, prosperous and happy, in that England which I shall see no more. I see her with a child upon her bosom, who bears my name. I see her father, aged and bent, but otherwise restored, and faithful to all men in his healing office, and at peace; I see the good old man, so long their friend in ten years' enriching them with all he has, and passing tranquilly to his reward.

"I see that I hold a sanctuary in their hearts, and in the hearts of their descendants, generations hence. I see her, an old woman, weeping for me on the anniversary of this day. I see her and her husband, their course done, lying side by side in their last earthly bed, and I know that each was not more honored and held sacred in the other's soul, than I was in the souls of both.

"I see (their) child . . . who bore my name, a man winning his way up in that path of life which once was mine. I see him winning it so well, that my name is made illustrious there by the light of his. I see the blots I threw upon it, faded away. I see him, foremost of just judges and honored men, bringing a boy of my name, with a forehead that I know and golden hair, to this place—then fair to look upon, with not a trace of this day's disfigurement ‹ and I hear him tell the child my story, with a tender and a faltering voice. "

Carton's sacrifice must have gained the approval of the Master himself who, some centuries before, had said, "Greater love hath no man than this, that a man lay down his life for his friends. " (John 15:13) This sacrifice for others was the best of Sydney Carton, but it was also the best of Jesus of Nazareth, as He made the great Atonement by laying down His own life that other people may live more happily forever.

Just before Sydney Carton's neck was placed upon the block to receive the axe, his last earthly utterance was, "It is a far, far better thing that I do, than I have ever done; it is a far, far better rest that I go to, than I have ever known. " This last day of the life of Sydney Carton was his best day. Nearly 200 years later, Winston Churchill said of a group of English airmen who were offering their lives for the same countries so loved by Mr. Dickens, "If the British Commonwealth and Empire shall last for a thousand years, yet men shall say (of these airmen) this was their finest hour. "

This attitude of doing great and noble service can make even death itself seem very pleasant. All of us in our lifetime reach certain comparative high points of accomplishment where we feel a sense of pride in what we have done, that at least in this one thing, our own lives have been outstandingly worthwhile. In the case of Mr. Carton, he not only did a great thing for the benefactor whose life he saved, but he also did a great thing for many millions of readers who have read this inspiring story and been uplifted by his deeds of courage, heroism, and sacrifice.

When I look at my copy of A *Tale of Two Cities* sitting there on the shelf, instead of it merely being a book, I think of it as containing the essence, the toil, the tears, and the sufferings of a great many human beings who were trying to do the best they could. I don't need to concern myself with discouragement, ignorance, and the sins of those who did wrong. Instead, I can be uplifted and inspired by the heroism and high purpose of those who did right. When I read of Mr. Dickens saying that he himself liked his great book A *Tale of Two Cities* more than any other of his famous works, the thought comes across that he is saying, "This is the best of me. "

So it is with other great authors as their most noteworthy deeds are recorded. I follow this procedure with the rest of my library, which is not merely a collection of books; rather it is a collection of great human beings endowed for my benefit with a kind of everlasting immortality. I draw from them the best of each one as his service is needed by me.

Like Sydney Carton, all of these great men and women may have set down in writing only the best one percent of themselves. Yet, it is in my books where they reach their great height of power, usefulness, and inspiration. It is as though each one of them had engraved in gold the statement, which would last forever, saying, "This is the best of me. " For the rest of these men's lives, they may have eaten and drunk and slept and loved and hated like other people; but in writing their books for me to read, each one says to me, "This is my very best. This is the greatest of what I saw, knew, believed, and did during my lifetime. If anything of mine is worth your memorizing and remembering, this is it. "

The compilers and publishers of these great books have put the best of many men together into a composite. The contribution of each may be brief in itself, but whatever he may have possessed of inspiration, dedication, and righteousness now belongs to me, without the necessity of taking anything from him which is ordinary. There are other ways to amplify and carry the voice, but my personal library eternally preserves the intellect, the ambition, and even the character itself of many of the greatest men and women for my benefit.

Each author had something to say which he perceived to be true and useful and helpfully beautiful. So far as he knew, no one had ever put it that way before. Perhaps no one else can say it the way he said it. That was his call, and he was bound to say it clearly, melodiously, and helpfully. Through the great books, the great scriptures, and the great poems, we may talk with the kings and queens of intellect and spirit so that we can more fully satisfy ourselves that our prayers for high companionship and exaltation of soul will be fully answered. It is not necessary to jostle with the common crowds for an entry here or an audience there, because all of the while this high, eternal, intellectual court is open to us with its society as wide as the world, and as multitudinous as all of its day. We may have fellowship and rank with the chosen and mighty of every place and time according to our own wish.

If we want to be the companions of nobles, all we need to do is to make ourselves noble, that we may understand what they are saying to our minds. The influence of great books upon us is miraculous. They can make us into their own image. And you may judge a man more truly by the books and the papers that he reads than by the social companions that he keeps. We do not need to lack for conversation with the wise.

If we understand wisdom, we shall hear it on every hand. We have only one limitation, and that is, if we do not rise to them, they cannot stoop to us.

In this book are presented qualities of outstanding great lives from many walks of life that include great poets, statesmen, philosophers, and warriors, headed by the Prince of Peace himself. If you listen carefully, each will say to you, "This is the best of me!"

YOUR OWN BIOGRAPHY

There are a great many very important tasks that everyone ought to do between the day of his birth and the day of his death. One of these is to write his autobiography to be included in his own hall of fame. The greatest commodity in the universe is life and a biography is a written history of life. However, there is a certain timeliness and permanence that can multiply the value and strengthen the effectiveness of a written biography, particularly when the biography strengthens one's own self- image and increases his general prestige.

Some people make a personal financial accounting by waiting until the month or the year is over and then compiling a summary of where their money went. There is a more effective budget system that involves making a program beforehand to determine where the money is to be spent, and then a follow-up to ensure the accuracy. A planned program that gives an autobiography its direction in real time is much more profitable than a story which, after death, merely recounts what happened.

17

The science of crime detection says that no one can pass through a room without leaving evidence of someone having been there. It may merely be a footprint, a scent, or a fallen hair, but there will be evidence somewhere that someone passed through the room. And what could be a more thrilling experience than to leave many pleasant evidences all around that the world is richer and more beautiful because you lived in it?

It is interesting that the subject we probably know less about than any other in the world is our own individual selves. You can ask a man questions about science, invention, history, or politics, and he will answer you. But, if you ask him to sit down and write out an analysis of himself, and tell you about his mind and soul qualities, you may not get a very good answer. We have great authority over our possessions and our faculties. If I tell my eyes to close, they close. If I tell my finger to bend, it bends. If I give my feet an order, they obey. And when I get that kind of authority over my brain, my tongue, my self-image, and my enthusiasm, I may be well on my way toward great accomplishments.

An autobiography forces us to study ourselves. If it is thought about in advance, in connection with what others have done with their lives, it can make things happen that will be pleasing and profitable to us. Benjamin Franklin went to school for only two years, but his autobiography is one of the greatest pieces of literature in the world. He tells about the important part that writing things down had on his total success. The study of the biography of others, and writing down our determination about great ideas we discover therein, is how we make greatness in all of its forms permanent in ourselves. The ancient Egyptians embalmed the bodies of their great Pharaohs and other important men and stored them away in magnificent pyramids and other tombs. Through our great biographical books, we embalm the minds and personalities of our greatest men and women and give them a kind of immortality by having them live on in us and in our posterity.

We rarely get any more out of a thing than we put into it. One man reported that when he started out to study himself, he thought he was a rather unimpressive person. But, when he finished, he was very much more enthusiastic about himself. The fact is, that the two most important people in the world are God and you. And this is where our energy and focus should be increased as much as possible. One of the most important segments of education is the study of human lives and the most important of those human lives is our own. We ought to study it and make a record of it as we go along. We may also improve our own life as we learn of the events, the circumstances, and the successes of those to whom we look for inspiration and direction.

The great history, the great literature, the great loves, the great faith, the great ideals, and the great occupational successes are a part of individual biography. They are a part of what Emerson had in mind when he said, "We live in the lap of an immense intelligence. . . but each must take the steps that would bring him there. " We are a part of a kind of united order process, which makes all this intelligence belong to us if we accept life's invitation to accept the gift. Upon the stage of life, we may watch the activities of the good and the bad, and we may learn from both.

We talk a great deal about confessing our sins. We also overdo the process of confessing our inferiority. But, we must not slight our virtues, nor our strengths. After one man had told a religious official about his weaknesses the reply was, "Now take an equal time telling me about your virtues and your strengths. " The young man was a little startled. He was used to being scolded, suspected, questioned and double checked. Here was a man who was his friend, who was more interested in the thrilling, the inspiring, the uplifting, than he was in the sordid, the shocking, and the depraved. I know a very inspiring man who in his greeting usually says, "I know something good about you. " Everyone should write an autobiography in which he gives proper attention to the good things about his own possibilities.

RALPH WALDO EMERSON

*"No good idea
was ever allowed
to get away."*

F ew things could be more fascinating than to study the life
of a great thinker. Van Wyck Brooks wrote an interesting
study of the gifted American essayist and poet, Ralph Waldo
Emerson that he titled, *A Biography of an Inner Life*. Mr.
Brooks studied Emerson from every point of view possible. He
examined his philosophy, his methods of communication, his
problems, and his successes. With interesting clarity, he was
able to look inside Emerson's mind where the real reasons for
both success and failure are always found. The biography gives
a series of "portraits" of Emerson's thinking, his spirit, his
attitudes, his motivations, and his nobility. The more we find
out about greatness, the more we understand that it comes in
response to some deliberate effort. The more we study other
people, the more we discover that their problems often have a
family resemblance to our own.

Emerson's business was communication, both in
speaking and writing. It is interesting to think of earning a
living by putting ideas down on paper that people would be

willing to pay money for. This concept might stimulate us to think of selling the products of our own minds. We might put ourselves in the shoes of any writer who is just beginning and try to understand his feelings. How would you proceed to accomplish your hopes of being successful if you were just starting out in this type of career? It has been said that George Bernard Shaw wrote for nine years before his writing could support him. Meanwhile, his widowed mother paid his bills. Mr. Shaw said that he did not throw himself into the battle of life, he threw his mother in. It would be an interesting challenge to write down enough good ideas to entice someone else to be willing to provide us with our daily bread.

In the process of learning to write, Emerson also had some important problems that had to be surmounted. For example, he said that he had an unmanageable mind. It jumped abruptly from one thing to another. He said that he could no more manage his thoughts than he could manage thunderbolts. At times his brain would become a blank and leave his mind in a state of barrenness. Life seemed to him like a flash of light that was followed by long periods of darkness. Most of the time, it seemed as though the great electronic machine of his brain was refusing to work. Often, even with the greatest effort, not even a spark was produced. These periodic movements that took place in his brain were mysterious and ungovernable.

For every mind, including his, there are always some natural stimulants, and it is up to us to find them. It is important to know that, if skillfully handled, minds can be charged and trained and made productive. The problem, of course, is to find the right stimulants, and to learn the procedures of good mind management. To discover how to run our lives according to our own best interests is the problem everyone wants to solve, no matter what vocation we have chosen.

As one of his most profitable stimulants Emerson decided to keep a journal, and once began, he kept it up faithfully. In his journal he wrote down every thought, every helpful suggestion, and he recorded every success. Each day he collected in his journal his disjointed dreams, his mental reveries, and the fragments of all of the ideas that his mind was able to conceive. The act of writing an idea down improves both the idea and the mind. Bacon said, "Reading makes a full man, but writing makes an exact man." You have to think an idea through before you can write it down. And to write the idea down gives it form, exactness, and makes it visible. When one's ideas can be brought under the scrutiny of the eyes, the ideas can be more readily improved.

Mr. Emerson's journal also became the hive in which he stored the honey of his mind as the bees of his brain produced it. Once his ideas were written down, Emerson could then go back and review them again and again, with the idea of making needed improvements. As he visited with great ideas, every day he grew accustomed to their faces. He discovered among them a great many family resemblances, and some intriguing future possibilities were suggested. Then he measured their abilities and learned to arrange them a little more attractively. After he improved their dress, brightened their faces, and increased their muscle power, he was able to join them together in a more effective order. Almost always his ideas came in fragments, but he knew that the missing links would soon show up to make his thoughts complete.

Once snared by Mr. Emerson, no good idea was ever

allowed to get away. He not only wrote it down immediately, but he put it in his mental incubator so the idea itself could grow. He knew that ideas have a natural tendency to propagate. Each idea has the possibility of an extensive posterity, and ideas come from parents just as people do. With all of these laws working in his favor, Emerson became a great man, a great thinker, a great communicator, and a great writer. His journal was very valuable, and he knew that even his unused thoughts would fit somewhere into an effective pattern of expression. He worked incessantly. He said, "Of all the tonics, work is the most effective." Emerson made the most of his natural success instincts, and he developed a good set of those work passions that became the causes of his labor.

Emerson trained his emotions and used them to motivate his will and give sufficient power to his ambitions. There was great inspiration for Emerson in any assertion of his own will. Every personality needs an emotional generator to set industry in motion. He believed in his work. He told himself that his particular work was the most inviting of all the forms of labor. He would thrill over a new phrase, which at times was like a torch applied to a train of powder. It awakened so many other thoughts, all of which he graded, sized, and put away in his incubator.

Brave words filled him with the cheerfulness of spring. They made his heart dance and quickened his brain. He beheld shining relationships between all things. When this excitement was in his mind, his enthusiasm impelled him to write. It almost impelled him to sing. After having once reached this productive state, he would not allow anything to throw him out of harmony. He allowed no discords to disrupt him because he found out how easy it was to "lapse into flesh and sleep. " He knew that a lapsed enthusiasm, or a lapsed hope, or a lapsed ambition was a useless and dead thing which could not easily be brought back to life. Therefore, Emerson kept things alive by keeping them moving.

The sight of a man of accomplishment filled him with boundless confidence in his own power. He studied men. He absorbed their ideas and their enthusiasms, and extracted their success. When thoughts refused to come, and the gift of the happy phrase and the bright image seemed to vanish forever, he did not merely sit and wait for it to return. Rather, he immediately began to write. He found he could bring on any spirit by the right kind of work. And with a period of effective work, he was soon floating off again on the most cordial tide of expression.

Emerson enjoyed many of those pleasant hours when things sailed through his head with little effort. The bright words came spontaneously like the breath of the morning wind. Then he could hardly sit in his chair for joy. Great ideas made him bolt upright or sent him striding about the room. On some occasions, he became so thrilled that he could not get a firm enough hold on his composure even to enable him to set down on paper the thoughts that excited him. On these occasions, his intellect was so active that everything ran out to meet it. He was like the maple trees in the spring when the sugar sap flows so fast that it is difficult to get enough tubs to contain it.

However, Emerson also had hours of painful sterility, and the feeling of a listless weariness. How could he ever learn to control these moods which did not even believe in each other? In one state of mind he never seemed able to remember or conceive of the opposite state. In the hours of mental sterility, it was difficult to remember the hours of abundant fertility. Sometimes he would go for days fighting his own skepticism. But fortunately, when things seemed to go wrong, he didn't quit. He learned that sooner or later the proper mood always returned.

Emerson felt that minds were like his pear trees which, after ten barren seasons, burst again into a second and even more glorious growth. However, he knew that these barren hours in himself must be avoided. He must steer clear of these mental allergies and natural work poisons which caused him sterility and barrenness. So far as all practical purposes were concerned, the things that distracted him were as bad as the things that crippled or stunned him. He had to get rid of all negative thoughts.

It was the Master who said, "If thy right eye offend thee, pluck it out . . . " (Matt. 5:29) This is still good counsel. All agents of disharmony must be destroyed, and nothing should be allowed to break one's constructive moods or cause distractions. Emerson wrote out his own great statement on this idea saying, "The one good in life is concentration; the one evil is dissipation. '' His goal was to write; and when he allowed himself to do a lot of unrelated things, he lost the spirit of his work. Domestic chores, parties, arguments, any other menial tasks disquieted him. There were hysterical, nervous persons who produced those same symptoms in him. To break the success mood and lose the spirit of accomplishment puts one on the road to failure.

The one who wants to write should write and not allow his enthusiasm to be diluted, or thwarted, or dissipated, or scattered, or killed. Manual labor distracted Emerson. His was the work of the spirit. He believed that writing was the greatest and most miraculous of the arts, and he felt unable to do his best when he had his pen in one hand and a crowbar or a peat knife in the other. He had heard of people saying, "Take life as it comes. " This was an unintelligible concept to Emerson. He believed that everyone should select his own good and tune out everything else. He had no place in his life for those success poisons and other discords that always drew him downhill. He believed in eliminating immediately all of those things, which weakened his enthusiasm or distorted his attitude. He found that the slightest irregularities in his program disturbed that delicate poise demanded by effective composition.

How ridiculous is he who, while trying to accomplish some great work, is always allowing his productive attitudes to be interrupted by a multitude of avoidable trifles. One is often equally interested in a hundred things instead of one thing. The thoughts which dilute one's mind may seem small to some, and yet it is the weight of these accumulated "feathers" on the scale that often tips the balance in favor of failure. Therefore, instead of accepting life as it came, Emerson would relieve himself from the possible confusion in his affairs by selecting for himself only those things which would carry him toward his one goal and eliminating everything else. He would meet every situation only on his own terms. And he always kept his goal in his mind before him.

Discord always produces deformity, and Emerson was horrified by the apathy which so often possessed him. This apathy is sometimes as dangerous as the numbness that precedes the death of a freezing man. Emerson knew that he must always keep moving if he was to maintain his health and reach his goals. He had to break the stranglehold of this natural inertia, and he had to rid himself of everything that was holding him back. It is necessary for one to get all contrary things out of the system before success can be enticed to stay.

The sand must be emptied out of the bucket if something more important is to be put in. Everyone seeking success should be skilled in the use of some good mental and spiritual purgatives. Certain bad habits and unhealthy attitudes must be flushed out before there is room for success. Emerson discovered that he could best advance his own interests by adopting some of the success patterns already developed by other people. Although many were tailor-made to fit him, it was only when the best in others was added to his own successful experience that he became what so many people considered to be one of the greatest thinkers that America has ever produced.

One of the amazing things about our human nature is that so few people ever consistently follow their own success pattern, or a success pattern developed by other men. Woodrow Wilson once said that a common characteristic of the American people was their ability to resist instruction. A great man writes out in detail those directions which exactly mark the path of success, and then we insist on maintaining our own mediocrity by disregarding the instructions and permitting ourselves to make most of the mistakes personally. Emerson was successful only because he did those definite things which success always demands of those who would win her favor. Some of these might be summarized as follows:

1. Concentrate.
2. Get the spirit of our particular success.
3. Clean out all discords.

4. Practice self-control.
5. Meet life on terms made to your order.
6. Domesticate those prolific periods of fertility.

Concentration requires that we cease the miscellaneous activities of our lives that have little or no meaning and only serve to divert our attention from our goal or project. Once we have done this, a spirit of success can be more fully embraced. Discords must also be eliminated so that we can stay the course and not deplete our energy. Self control is then the key to obtaining that which we have set out to gain. Meeting life on our own terms means we must entertain only those thoughts and experiences that will help us. Don't take into your minds all of the fears, doubts, sins, and distractions that will hinder your cause. On the radio network of causes, don't try to pick up simultaneously every program that is on every station. Most importantly, when the periods of creativity, of energy, and of resolute determination hit us, it is time to capitalize on these powerful forces and maintain the momentum for as long as possible. Shakespeare said, "There is a tide in the affairs of men which, taken at its flood, leads on to fortune; omitted, all of the voyages of our lives are bound in shallows and in miseries. On such a full sea are we now afloat, and we must take the current when it serves or lose our ventures."

We should also remember that there will come periods that are comparatively barren and unfruitful. When these periods arrive, never get depressed and quit trying. If you focus, if you are consistent and keep working, the spirit of success will soon return. Emerson had tonics for his mind which he could use when it seemed that he had lost his power. He had a healthy, vigorous philosophy of life. He developed his emotions and attitudes, and deliberately built up those motivating emotional currents that set off his industry.

Each of us has a set of invisible tools with which we may fashion greater mental power. It is largely these strong internal forces to which Mr. Van Wyke Brooks referred as "Emerson's inner life. " These powers determined his success, and with the same kind of development, they can also determine ours. Should we feel lacking or weak and in need of extra help, we have no further to look then to the lives of great men and women who have gone before us and who have trod the path for us to follow. Seek their wisdom that it may be yours.

WINSTON CHURCHILL

"I felt as though I was walking with destiny . . ."

O n May 10th, 1940, Winston Churchill, then age sixty-six, became Prime Minister of England. This was the time when the powerful German air force was making round-the-clock trips across the English Channel dumping planeload after planeload of bombs on England. No one knew whether the British would be able to hold out for another week or a month.

England had already been badly mauled by the conquering Germans. What General Weygand had called the "Battle of France" was over. The Continental countries had already fallen into German hands. Everyone knew the survival of Christian civilization depended upon the outcome of the furious Battle of Britain.

Churchill was not involved in any of the humiliating mistakes that had previously been made trying to appease the aggressors. On the contrary, he had always vigorously opposed any appeasement of evil men. And he was the one statesman who had dared to state the truth about the weak and shameful compromises at Munich at a time when everybody else was hugging the fading illusions of peace.

This devastating policy of giving in to evil had been referred to as providing "peace for our time. " But Churchill had a habit of calling things by their proper names. Speaking of Munich, he said, "The people should know that we have sustained a defeat without war. They should know that we have passed an awful milestone in our history. The whole equilibrium of Europe has now been deranged, and these terrible words have (for the time being) been pronounced against the Western democracies, saying 'Thou art weighed in the balances and are found wanting. '"

Churchill said, "And do not suppose that this is the end. This is only the beginning of the reckoning. This is only the first foretaste of a bitter cup which will be proffered to us year after year unless by a supreme recovery of our moral health and martial vigor, we shall arise and again take our stand for freedom as in the olden time. "

When the opportunity came with all of its mortal danger, Churchill was able to express the nation's will to resist as no one else could. Even before that critical day of May 10th, everyone knew that there had to be some new blood in the government if the world was to be saved at all. They had to have someone who would stand up for the right instead of following the weak course of trying to appease criminals and making unsatisfactory deals with evil.

Winston Churchill was that man. For in no one did the fires of freedom burn with a brighter flame than in this rugged old Englishman. Therefore, on May 10th, 1940, the burdens of a great groggy empire were dumped upon the shoulders of this one man. To him was given the job of nearly single handedly winning the war. How would you feel about such an assignment if it were placed upon your shoulders?

It might be inspiring to know how Winston Churchill felt. He said: "As I went to bed at about 3:00 a. m. , I was conscious of a profound feeling of relief. At last I had authority to give direction over this whole scene. And I felt as though I were walking with destiny that my past life had been but a preparation for this hour, for this trial. I could not be reproached either for having made the war or for lack of preparation for it. But I felt that I knew a good deal about it and I was sure I would not fail. " Fail to do what? Fail to save the world from the greatest mechanized might ever known, and with a minimum of equipment and men!

Amid the failures and defeats of 1756, the elder William Pitt declared, "I know that I can save my country and that no one else can. " That spirit of substantiated self-confidence made its reappearance in Winston Churchill amid the shattering events of 1940. Fortunately for the free world, England had a great resource unmatched in any other nation– they had Winston Churchill.

Churchill had many great qualities. He was always at his best when fighting against overwhelming odds. The appeasers had said, "Nothing is worse than war. " But with the full organ of his voice, supported by the magnificent courage of his great spirit, Churchill boomed back, "Dishonor is worse than war, and slavery is worse than war. "

In three days' time he had organized the government which he was to head, and England was on her way to victory. He went before the House of Commons and in his first speech as prime minister, on May 13, 1940, he said, "You ask, what is our policy? I will tell you. It is to wage war. It is to wage war by sea, by land and in the air with all our might and with all the strength that God can give us. To wage war against a monstrous tyranny never surpassed in the dark lamentable catalogue of human crime. That is our policy.

"You ask what is our aim? I can answer in one word–victory–victory at all costs, victory in spite of all the terror, victory however long and hard the road may be, for without victory there is no survival–no survival for the urge and impulse of the ages. But, I take up my task with buoyancy and hope, I feel sure that our cause will not be suffered to fail among men. "

Then he went on the radio to arouse the people of the empire. And in closing his speech on June 4, 1940, he said, "We shall not flag nor fail. We shall go on to the end. We shall fight in France. We shall fight on the seas and the oceans. We shall fight with growing confidence and power in the air, we shall defend our island whatever the cost of it may be. We shall fight on the beaches. We shall fight on the landing grounds. We shall fight in the fields and in the streets. We shall fight in the hills. We shall never surrender and even if, which I do not for a moment believe, this Island or a large part of it were subjugated and starving, then our Empire beyond the seas, armed and guarded by the British fleet would carry on the fight until in God's own time the new world in its power and might steps forth to the rescue and the liberation of the old. "

It was not long before the marvelous courage and inspiring eloquence of this amazing man stirred up similar feelings in those who listened. On June 18, 1940, he said, "Hitler knows that he will have to break us in this Island or lose the war. If we can stand up to him, all Europe may be free, and the life of the world may move forward into the broad sunlit uplands. But if we fail, then the whole world, including the United States, including all that we have known and cared for, will sink into the abyss of a new Dark Age made more sinister and perhaps more protracted by the light of perverted science. Let us therefore brace ourselves that, if the British Empire and its Commonwealth shall last for a thousand years, men will say this was their finest hour. "

With this kind of spiritual eloquence and personal power, the tide of the war soon began to change. While reviewing the first year of the war, before the House of Commons, he said, "The gratitude of every home in our Island, in our Empire, and indeed throughout the world, except in the abodes of the guilty, goes out to the British airmen who undaunted by odds, unwearied in their constant challenge and mortal danger, are turning the tide of the war by their prowess and devotion. Never in the field of human conflict have so many owed so much to so few. "

All of the people in the world will always owe an enormous debt, not only to the British airmen, but also to their great Prime Minister. And when the history books are written covering this time period, the man who will stand above all others will be Winston Churchill. His life was distinguished by many things; one of them was character. In the corresponding years of his political life, even his worst enemies have never once intimated that he was a liar, or unfair, or immoral, or dishonorable. He was not lazy, nor weak, nor afraid. He was not burdened down with any records of failure, guilt, or inferiority. He was the greatest statesman of the 20th Century. He was also its greatest orator. He is now hailed as the greatest parliamentarian of modern times and probably of all time. He stands preeminent among all of the great men of his age and is high on the list among the giants of world history.

In the early 1940's, President Franklin D. Roosevelt wrote to Churchill and said, "It is fun to live in the same decade with you. " It is not only fun to live alongside great men, it is also very profitable. In him we see a picture of rugged, dogged determination with the ability to overcome every difficulty placed in his way. We cannot imagine Churchill believing in or tolerating weakness in himself.

He was a master of descriptive journalism and the greatest national hero of his time. He had a mastery of both written and spoken words that is attained by very few men. His skill as an organizer and administrator is well known. He was a man of extraordinarily strong convictions. Churchill was a master of argument and debate. He was a formidable opponent. His intensity of purpose made his delivery seem natural and appropriate. He used humor and pathos with equal facility. And for quotation, he drew on everything from the Greek classics to Donald Duck. He supported his position with interesting clichés, forceful slang, as well as holy writ.

Churchill was a warrior, yet his recreations were painting and bricklaying. However, the master strain of his character was that of a rhetorician. Churchill used words with the same daring and abandon that he did colors. Whether painting or speaking, he daubed it on boldly and recklessly.

His command of the beauty and imagery which reside in the English language was always manifested. He used to delight the House of Commons with his magnificent epigrams and great sense of humor. Never once did the most skillful socialist swordsman ever get under his guard in parliament. He prepared his speeches with great care because he very properly believed that the House had a right to expect that he would perform at his best, and that the fate of a nation should not be entrusted in the hands of weaklings, cowards, or those who were sick in spirit. Someone once humorously said of Churchill that he realized that he was not omniscient, but he often pretended that he was. It was said that he did not study to make himself a demagogue; he was born a demagogue and he happened to know it. President Roosevelt said, "Churchill has a hundred ideas a day of which at least four are good ones. Moreover he does not forget what he has read, and since he reads a lot, he is a walking reference library. This fact gives him an incredible amount of time to use for other things. " Churchill took the time to become the master of whatever he was doing. He was always in the forefront in appearance, in manner, in dress and above all other things, in his speech. He often squeezed the last ounce out of the English language, his unique command of which is one of his most persuasive gifts. Even more fundamental was his meticulous study of any subject under discussion. With great care and patience, he built up his case. He read every document to be found on the subject; and with Churchill, to read was to remember. Few men have ever had a greater capacity for assimilating facts. He was never known to go into a conference with an ill- prepared or half- digested case. He knew when he entered a cabinet or a committee meeting what he wanted done, and he always had a plan to bring about the right solution.

Churchill had a brilliant depth of thought, a great breadth of view, an inspiring philosophy of life, and a fine knowledge of human nature. But his chief gift, his primary asset, was his facility of expression. He was master of the two-fold logos, the thought and the word. They are distinct, but they are inseparable from each other. He always had the right word for the right idea and he never had a word too much. If he was brief it was because a few words would suffice. If he was lavish, each word still hit its mark and aided the vigorous march of his elocution. He expressed what all felt, but which all could not say. His sayings passed into proverbs among the people, and his phrases have become household words and idioms in their daily speech. With Churchill it was not merely the things that he said that counted, it was the character of the man that breathed them into his sentences.

Many of Churchill's speeches made history. They changed the shape of events. They shed a clearer light upon the path of duty, and they implanted in ordinary men and women the resolve to make that day of danger their finest hour. He brought triumph out of the jaws of defeat by appealing to the noblest and deepest feelings of mankind, even while discouragement and despair besieged their hearts.

In a talk that Churchill gave at the beginning of the war in *The Free Trade Hall*, he said, "Come then, let us to the task, to the battle, to the toil– each to our part, each to our station. Fill the armies, rule the air, pour out the munitions, strangle the U-boats, sweep the mines, plough the land, build the ships, guard the streets, succor the wounded, uplift the downcast and honor the brave. " Whether a speech is simple or ornate, a great orator must have a profound sense of the value of words in their right order. Their meaning and rhythm can be given the power to make a magic appeal.

Words are the raw materials of all speeches. They have a life of their own. They have color, sound, quality, and a meaning that comes from association. The great masters of language can give them a use that Montague called "the glamorous prestige of high adventure in great company. " If you take a few words and effectively put them together they may flash into life in a powerful sentence, a beautiful song, an inspiring revelation, or some other new creation that may remain a joy forever.

Churchill possessed this supreme gift. He chose the right word, not only for its sound, but also with an instinctive knowledge of its decorative and emotional meaning. He said, "The fact that the British Empire stands invincible. . . will kindle again the spark of hope in the breasts of hundreds of millions of downtrodden and despairing men and women throughout Europe and far beyond its bounds. And from these sparks there will presently come a cleansing and a devouring flame. Death and sorrow will be the companions of our journey; hardship will be our garment, constancy and valor will be our only shield. We must be united. We must be undaunted, we must be inflexible. Our qualities and deeds must burn and glow through the gloom of Europe until they become the veritable beacon of its salvation. We shall not fail or falter; we shall not weaken or tire. Neither the sudden shock of battle, nor the long-drawn trials of vigilance and exertion will wear us down. " He said, "Just give us the tools and we will finish the job. "

GEORGE WASHINGTON CARVER

*"The American with
the worst start and
the best finish-no alibis."*

Henry Ford once said that Dr. Carver was the greatest living scientist since the death of Thomas A. Edison. However, that was far from his greatest achievement. George Washington Carver shares with Booker T. Washington the honor of having been a predominate force in improving the lives of African- Americans and in creating a more favorable racial understanding. One of his most important contributions was that the fame of his achievements undermined the widespread stereotype of the time that the black race was intellectually inferior to the white race.

If we were to choose an American who had the worst start and the best finish in his life, it might well be George Washington Carver. George was born into slavery on a cold January night in 1864 before a little fire in a slave hut in Diamond Grove, Missouri. His father was a slave from another plantation who was killed before his son was born. His mother was owned by Moses Carver who, while he did not personally approve of slavery, took advantage of the custom of the times

41

to supply his household and plantation with domestic help.

The story goes that Moses Carver paid $700 for a thirteen-year old slave girl by the name of Mary. Six years later she had given birth to a son whom she named George. He was a sickly child from the time of his birth. When George was only six weeks old, he and his slave mother were stolen by a group of plundering night raiders and carried into Arkansas.

Sometime after the kidnapping, a rumor reached Moses Carver that a man named John Bentley knew the whereabouts of Mary and her baby, and he would agree to try to steal them back if given a substantial reward. Mary seemed like one of the family, so Moses sent for the man and said, "Go after them, Bentley. I haven't much money, but I will give you forty acres of my best timberland and my best horse to bring Mary and her baby back."

After a few days, Bentley returned with a bundle wrapped in his coat tied to the back of the saddle. He handed it over to Mrs. Carver, saying doubtfully, "I guess it's still alive." He had found little George in the care of another woman, but there was no sign of Mary. One report said that she was dead. Another said that she had been taken to Louisiana. But apparently whoever had taken her did not want to be bothered with the baby, whom they abandoned. Mary was never heard of again.

George assumed the Carver's name and remained with them until he was ten years old. He was always sickly, stammered badly, and half of the time no one could understand what he was trying to say. Yet even at that young age, he kept constantly at work, regardless of how he felt. He was always alone, but was never lonely. He talked to the horses, the trees, and the flowers. He accepted his lot without whining, although he sometimes thought that a mule was more fortunate than he, because the mule could feel only the white man's blows on his body, not those on his spirit. Young George learned that self-pity is a destructive force, and if he could only learn to stand the blows which he received, they would help him to develop and assist him on his way to success.

George loved plants, and even as a boy he became known as "The Plant Doctor. " Dying plants seemed to revive more quickly under his care. Any opportunity to work around plants and flowers he eagerly accepted. He wanted to learn about things. He thirsted for something that seemed beyond him, and whenever he saw an opportunity that tended to satisfy that thirst for more knowledge, he automatically moved in that direction. He could not go to school like white children, but he was permitted to attend a Sunday school which was held before the regular church service. Afterwards, he would sit on the steps and listen to the singing and absorb whatever he could hear of what was said inside.

Even as a little boy he had a very studious nature. From his position on the outside of the church, he got a small taste of the fruit of knowledge and caught a glimpse of the mysteries hidden in words and ideas. He could no longer be content. George looked with longing at the doors of the school house that were closed to him, but he announced to himself that someday he was going to have a school of his own, just as he had a nursery for sick plants.

George had a great passion for education and for the chance to teach others of his race. He wanted to free their minds, as Lincoln had freed their bodies. And so, at age 10, he placed his own bare feet on the road to knowledge, leaving the Carver's to go where he could be closer to an opportunity

43

for learning. The Carver's, recognizing George's gifts and ambitions, allowed him to go his own way, feeling even then that he would accomplish something in the world if allowed to follow his natural talents.

The next few years, though filled with the most distressing poverty, were years of great accomplishment for George. He seemed to come naturally by integrity and honor. He had no inclination to cheat or lie. He did not need to be taught industry or self-reliance. Life had done that for him. He was like a sponge thirsting for more knowledge that was increased by the salt of fervor. A huge, insatiable question mark had been in his mind ever since he could think at all. The controlling motive of his life was that he wanted to know. He fed his mind constantly, yet it was never satisfied. His continual exclamation of, "I want to know," was followed by its corollary, "I can do that." These two statements combined to perfect the dynamo that powered his life. When he saw someone do something with their hands, he felt he could do it also.

George gave no thought to working his way through school. He had always worked his way through everything. He reminded himself that one could make money and lose it, but no one could take his education away from him. He knew he had a great future in store, and he resolved to prepare for it thoroughly.

Extremely hard years followed the proclamation of freedom for slaves, which said, "By the irrevocable action of this convention, slavery is abolished in the State of Missouri now and forever. None hereafter shall know any master but God," Yet these were days of great humiliation and suffering for those who had been freed.

George was naturally sensitive and shy, yet he never spoke of the wounds he suffered to his pride or his dignity as a human being. He felt that there were so many people in the world who were pleasant and kind and helpful that he did not have time to pay any attention to those who were not. He said, "Why waste time getting so disturbed that I can accomplish nothing. "

He instinctively disliked a man who was ashamed of his color. George didn't try to be someone else. He didn't want to be someone else. He simply wanted to be what he was, and make the most of himself, and help others of his own race. His own importance was because of what he could do for someone else. He said, "I must take better care of myself. I realize that God has a work for me to do and consequently I must be careful of my health. "

George possessed high ethical standards and religious principles. He believed in carrying the Bible in his heart, not merely under his arm. Some people have too much religion and not enough Christianity. They have too much creed and not enough performance. The world is perishing for want of kindness. But when people humiliated him, he only said, "Never mind, they don't understand. It doesn't make any difference. " George had a wonderful attitude about others. He also had a good attitude about himself. When he wrote letters, he always signed himself, "Your humble servant in God. " This relationship he did not take lightly.

He finally graduated with high honors from Iowa College in the field of agriculture in 1894. Then it was not long before he achieved his ambition of becoming a teacher. He had done so well that he was made a member of the Iowa College faculty. There is no doubt that it is a gift of a truly great teacher to see possibilities in others before the pupils themselves are conscious that they exist; and George tried to bring out the best traits in others, as he had done in himself. A strong inclination to learn and achieve, aided by necessity and an unflagging persistence, had produced this Carver phenomena of excellence.

He made no alibis. An excuse was useless. It was only one of the ways of saying, "You just didn't get the job done. " When George undertook a task, you could rest assured that the job would be done. He was a lover of dependability. Someone said, "Just get George to make a promise and then you can rest easy. It will be completed. " This was the reputation that he had built up, and this was the quality he tried to instill in other people. He said, "Get the drone out of you. Remember the more ignorant we are, the less use God has for us. "

He was thoroughly impatient with dabblers. Each student had to complete what he had started. He would say to the student, "I will help you as long as you are making progress. But once you decide to quit, I will not waste my time any further, and don't take up any of my time with a frivolous excuse. All I want to know is, is the thing done?"

In his early school days, he had been shown a picture that had been painted by someone they had called an "artist. " He was greatly impressed that an artist could make this beautiful picture with his hands. This thought took possession of George, and he kept repeating the words, "He made it with his hands. I want to do that. " After this experience, George was always drawing. He had nothing to draw with; but whenever he found a blank space on a stone, or a board, or even on the ground, he scratched something on it. He made colors out of poke berries, roots, and barks, and painted on cans, wooden pails, pieces of glass – anything.

But his real life's work began in 1896 when Booker T. Washington invited him to come to Tuskegee as head of the Department of Agriculture. Many of his students were like children, even though fully grown. He worked with them individually. He watched their natural inclination and the way they walked; then, he put paths under their feet.

George Washington Carver made over 300 products from the common peanut, 118 out of the sweet potato, and 75 from the pecan nut. With his knowledge of chemistry and physics, he took these apart, separated the water, fats, oils, gums, resins, sugars, starches, pectoses, pentasans, and amino acids. Then when he had all of the parts spread out before him, he put them back together in different ways. He realized that farms could be transformed into something more than food factories; they could become a source of raw materials for industry.

Some of the products made from the peanut included beverages, flour, coffee, salve, bleach, paint remover, wood filler, washing powder, metal polish, paper, ink, plastic, shaving cream, rubbing oil, linoleum, shampoo, axle grease, and synthetic rubber. Peanut milk, which would not curdle when cooked or when acids were added, and which contained all the elements of cow's milk, was discovered, along with cream that would rise upon it and could be turned into butter without souring. Peanut milk contained three and one-half times as much cheese as cow's milk.

He made leather stains, fruit punch, quinine, thirty different kinds of dies, face cream as soft as any almond cream, and a massage to fatten infants which was much more readily absorbed by the skin than olive oil. Peanut flour contained more than four times as much protein and eight times as much fat as wheat flour. He invented medicines from peanuts and made a more effective peat moss from peanut shells. George also discovered that the peanut is almost equal to sirloin steak for proteins, the potato for carbohydrates, and was inferior only to butter in fat. It was no wonder George earned a clear right to the title applied to him of "The Wizard of Tuskegee. "

Dr. Carver was in great demand throughout the Southern states, and also in the north, to give lectures. Usually he was not allowed to sleep in "white hotels" or even eat at "white luncheons. " He would be kept waiting in some other room until the luncheon was over, and then he would be brought in to give his lecture. His many trips were usually a curious mixture. While he was in transit to or from a place of meeting, he sometimes experienced extreme discomfort, both physical and mental, with a strange irony he could never escape. He was forced to sit in a big public lobby or in a hotel, longing for a place to rest, while the management was deciding he would not be admitted. But the very next day, while he was on the platform speaking in this same hotel, he would receive the greatest acclaim, always from big crowds.

It seemed that no matter how carefully the numbers of his hearers had been estimated in advance, the hall chosen was seldom large enough. Often there were more outside than in. Charmed with his knowledge, his dry humor and whimsicalities, audiences listened and marveled. He did, however, often run the risk of being mobbed by the very people he tried to help. No one ever found any harm in Dr. Carver. This treatment was only because of his color. This apparent injustice must have cut deeply such a naturally timid soul, but Dr. Carver used to say to his students, "If you have nothing but a complexion to recommend you, you have no recommendation. " And all through his hurts, he only said, "Never mind. They don't understand. It doesn't make any difference. "

Dr. Carver lived in the days of the Southern sharecropper when it was the popular thing to move onto the land, drain from it whatever fertility was possible, and then move on to some other place. Such a philosophy did more damage to the farmer than it did to the farm. One farmer said, "I have worn out three farms already. " This is one of the places where Dr. Carver made a great contribution, not only to the land, but also to the people who lived upon it. There are some people who will remember George Washington Carver because of his great educational effort among his race. Others will remember George Washington Carver because he made some 300 commercial products out of the common peanut. But, I will remember George Washington Carver because he said that every man owes it to himself to leave the soil a little richer than when he found it. That is what he did, not only to the soil, but to the lives of all of the people, both black and white, with whom he came in contact or who studied the philosophy of his life.

When he was asked why he had never married, he said that he had never had time. He died at Tuskegee on January 5, 1943. During his over eighty years of life, he had been honored by American presidents, statesmen, educators, and everyone who knew him. He became the benefactor of thousands of people who will never know his name. He had the worst start and made the best finish of anyone of his generation. That fact alone will inspire many others to make their own lives more productive.

LEONARDO DA VINCI

Saper Vedere
(knowing how to see)

Ralph Waldo Emerson once said that every great institution is the lengthened shadow of a man. The greatness of a nation or even of an age is written in the biographies of its heroic men and women. This earth has been particularly rich in the quality of its great people who, in giant form, have walked upon our planet. These famous names have come from such fields as religion, art, science, culture, business, and government, etc. One of these names, which some people place very near the top of the list, is the Italian genius, Leonardo da Vinci.

DaVinci was born the son of Ser Piero da Vinci on April 15, 1452. He died sixty-seven years later on May 2, 1519. His magnificent artistic talent brought him fame from all four corners of the earth. In 1963, one of his paintings, the *Mona Lisa*, was loaned by the French government to the American government to be displayed for a short period in Washington and New York. In both states the masterpiece attracted tremendous crowds. It was agreed, by those in charge, that they should insure the painting's safety during its round-trip journey. It was appraised for insurance purposes by a committee of competent appraisers at $100,000,000.

For some people it is difficult to understand how a painted canvas of $2^{1/2}$ by $3^{1/3}$ feet could be worth such a great sum. But if we think about it, there are many cases where a painted canvas has changed the entire lives of many people by drawing their ambitions and aspirations upward toward more worthwhile things. Leonardo da Vinci created this masterpiece, plus countless other priceless treasures, giving us some kind of idea of what his own life might have been appraised at. He certainly has influenced for good, in so many ways, the billions of people who have lived upon our planet.

Descriptions given by the patrons in Washington and New York about the *Mona Lisa* included such words as delightful, thrilling, and enchanting. John Walker, director of the National Gallery, who accompanied the *Mona Lisa* back to Paris, pointed out that more people came to see this painting than had ever attended a major football game, a famous prize fight, or a world series. The important thing, said Mr. Walker, was not how many people were attracted to her, but that she acted as a catalytic agent causing an aesthetic explosion in the minds of many of those who eyes fell upon her face.

In speaking at the opening of the exhibition, President John F. Kennedy said, "At the same time that Leonardo da Vinci, the creator of this painting, was opening up such a wide new world to Western civilization, his fellow countryman from Italy, Columbus, was opening up another new world by his discovery of America. The life of this painting here before us tonight, " said President Kennedy, "spans the entire life of the new world. We citizens of nations unborn at the time of its creation are among the inheritors and protectors of the ideals which gave it birth.

"Leonardo da Vinci was not only an artist and a sculptor, an architect and a scientist, but a military engineer, an occupation which he pursued, he tells us, in order to preserve the chief gift of nature, which is liberty. In this belief, he expresses the most profound premises of our own two nations. "

DaVinci's *Last Supper* is also one of the most famous paintings in the world. In its monumental simplicity, the composition of the scene is masterful; the power of its effect comes from the striking contrast in the attitudes of the young disciples as counter posed to Christ. Other masters, such as Rubens and Rembrandt, marveled at DaVinci's composition and were influenced by it. This painting has become widely known through countless reproductions and prints, the most important of those being produced by Raffaello Morghen in 1800. Thus, the *Last Supper* has become part of humanity's common heritage and remains today one of the world's outstanding paintings. This again increases DaVinci's contribution to all of the people living upon the earth.

However, more important than his pictures, or his machines or his pieces of sculpture, stands the man whom we look upon to draw ourselves upward. Giorgio Vasari spoke for millions of people when he said of DaVinci, "The heavens often rain down the richest gifts on human beings. But sometimes, with lavish abundance, they bestow upon a single individual beauty, grace, and agility, so that, whatever he does, every action is so divine that he surpasses all other men, and clearly displays how his genius is the gift of God and not an acquirement of human art. Men saw this in Leonardo da Vinci, whose personal beauty could not be exaggerated, whose very movement was grace itself, and whose abilities were so extraordinary that he could readily solve every difficulty. He possessed great personal strength, combined with dexterity, and a spirit and courage invariably royal and magnanimous; and the fame of his name so spread abroad that, not only was he praised in his own day, but his renown was greatly increased since his death. "

In addition to painting awe inspiring portraits, Leonardo da Vinci was a fine writer. He sang beautifully, accompanying himself on the lyre, and often sang songs of his own composition. As an engineer, DaVinci conceived ideas vastly ahead of his own time, conceptually inventing a helicopter, a tank, the use of concentrated solar power, a calculator, and many other ingenious plans. Very few of his designs were constructed or even possible during his lifetime. Some of his smaller inventions such as the automated bobbin winder entered the world of manufacturing unheralded.

One of the aspects of his life that seems equally inspiring, even with his greatest works, are the thousands of pages of illustrations, explanations, drawings, and writings which he produced. The depth and scope of these papers indicate the vast field where his mind had conceived and done much of its exploration. But unfortunately, the short years of his life left him insufficient time to complete a majority of his projects.

Nearly seven thousand pages from his notebooks exist today on which he sketched ideas and inventions, along with his notes, which show him to be a brilliant and original thinker.

It was during his years in Milan that DaVinci began the earliest of these notebooks. He would first make quick sketches of his observations on loose sheets or on tiny paper pads he kept in his belt. Then, he would arrange them according to theme and enter them in order in the notebook. In a sentence in the margin of one of his late anatomy sketches, he implores his "neighbors" to see that his works are printed.

An unusual feature in DaVinci's writings is the new function given to illustrate vis-à-vis the text. Leonardo strove passionately for a language that was clear yet expressive. The vividness and wealth of his vocabulary were the result of intense self-study and represented a significant contribution to the evolution of scientific prose in the Italian vernacular. On the other hand, in his teaching method, DaVinci gave absolute precedence to the illustration over the written word. Hence, the drawing does not illustrate the text, rather, the text serves to explain the picture. In formulating his own principle of graphic representation–which he himself called Dimostrazione—DaVinci was a precursor of modern scientific illustration.

To Leonardo da Vinci, sight was man's highest sense organ, because sight alone conveyed the facts of experience immediately, correctly, and with certainty. Hence, every phenomenon perceived became an object of knowledge. *Saper vedere* (knowing how to see) became the great theme of his studies of man's works and nature's creations. His creativity reached out into every realm in which graphic representation is used: he was a painter, sculptor, architect, and engineer. But, he went even beyond that. His superb intellect, his unusual power of observation, and his mastery of the art of drawing, unchecked by formal schooling, led him to the study of nature

itself, which he pursued with method and penetrating logic–
and in which his art and his science were equally revealed.

Over speculative book knowledge, which he scorned,
he set irrefutable facts gained from experience–from *saper
vedere* (knowing how to see). For DaVinci, the drawn image
was more precise than the written. One of the striking things
about the machines in some of his notebooks was how they
prefigure the future history of formal engineering draftsmanship
without becoming schematic diagrams. They were conceptions
rather than blueprints, but conceptions that one could take to
a factory and build tomorrow. Moreover, they were conceived
as a series and DaVinci was credited with being the inventor of
"modern scientific illustration."

Highly esteemed, DaVinci was constantly kept busy as
a painter, and sculptor, and as a designer of court festivals.
He was also frequently consulted as a technical adviser in the
fields of architecture, fortifications, and military matters.
And he served as a hydraulic and mechanical engineer. In this
phase of his life, DaVinci's genius unfolded to the fullest in all
of its versatility and creatively powerful artistic and scientific
thought, achieving that quality of uniqueness that called forth
the awe and astonished admiration of his contemporaries.
At the same time, in the boundlessness of the goals he set
himself, DaVinci's genius bore the mark of the unattainable so
that, if one traces the outlines of his lifework as a whole, one
is tempted to call it a grandiose unfinished symphony.

The immense range of his scientific studies is
unparalleled. It includes mathematics, optics, mechanics,
anatomy and physiology, zoology, botany, geology, and
paleontology. And the vision informing those studies was
just as impressive. His notes toward a treatise on the flight of

birds, for example, inspired him to consider a flying machine for man. He dreamed up the "worm gear," a key element in many machines that was invented again in the eighteenth century by clockmaker Henry Hindley.

DaVinci developed a simple frame to keep ball bearings from rubbing together; the frame was re-invented for use on vehicles in 1772. Another arrangement, in which ball bearings nestle around a conical pivot, was not re-created until the 1920's, when Sperry Gyroscope developed it for aircraft instruments—with no idea that DaVinci had thought of it first. In a sense, he even invented the bicycle. Some of his notebooks contain drawings of drive chains.

It was initially as an artist that DaVinci began his studies of the earth itself. For him the earth was a living organism, analogous to the human body. He also flirted with the law of action and reaction eventually stated by Newton, and his mind even danced around what later became Einstein's theory on the relationship between acceleration and gravity.

Certainly, Leonardo da Vinci was a man of superior mental power, endless originality, and incomparable industry. He did any one of a number of things which made his life outstanding. A million dollar *Mona Lisa*, or a several hundred million dollar *Last Supper* would have made the entire lives of many people outstanding, but Leonardo da Vinci went far beyond his painted masterpieces. The greatest amount of his work was left unfinished. His notebooks were lost and his ideas are still being rediscovered in our day. We might be intrigued by the thought of what DaVinci could have accomplished if he had been given capable associates and unlimited funds to bring his concepts to life.

Leonardo da Vinci understood the value of hard work

and the marvelous results of it when he declared, "Thou, Oh God, doth sell us all good things at the price of labor." DaVinci's life should serve as an example of our own productive potential. It should remind us of the need to write down on paper our ideas, our thoughts, our dreams, for they too can become a masterpiece with enough concentration and study. We live in a time of hurried accomplishment and instant gratification. Thus, we often miss the joy in life that comes from discovering our own talents, exercising our own minds, and exerting our own strength.

BENJAMIN FRANKLIN

A
Quest for Perfection

T he eighteenth century, which was destined to be the time when the greatest nation ever to live upon the earth was born, also produced a vast array of great men. Among these wise and spiritual men were our Founding Fathers, a specially selected group of men whom God raised up to give our nation the start toward its destiny. One of these superb men went by the name of Benjamin Franklin. He has been characterized by many people as one of the greatest men that our earth has ever produced. And he might serve us as the instrument to inspire our own ambition.

Probably the most important eight words in our language are these, "And God created man in his own image." Man, like God, was endowed with limitless possibilities and potentialities, and an innate hope that he might gain his fullest potential. Benjamin Franklin was one of these.

He was born January 17, 1706, in Boston, Massachusetts. He died eighty-four years later on April 17, 1790. He packed within those eighty-four years more successes in as many fields as any man or woman could ever achieve or hope to surpass.

He went to school for only two years and at age ten he was taken from school to assist his father as a candle maker and soap boiler. Later he was an apprentice to his brother, James, who was a printer. He signed a contract at age fourteen which was to be in effect until he turned twenty-one. He was to receive no pay except for the last year and his brother was obligated to pay for Ben's costs at a nearby boarding house. This left Ben with no money for the books that he craved. So one day he made a deal with his brother to give him half the board money and let him board himself. His brother was delighted, and Ben lived on one-half of his half of the boarding money and bought books with the balance.

Soon the apprentice agreement was cancelled because of his brother's financial problems, and Ben was permitted to go into business for himself. Throughout his life, in spite of his many prestigious accomplishments, he always delighted to identify himself as B. Franklin, Printer.

Benjamin Franklin took an oath to love the truth and help mankind. He was a great success as a man and as a journalist. Ben created a fictitious person he could quote, and named him Richard Saunders, whom he characterized as a poor, modest, but very wise person. For many years, he published *Poor Richard's Almanac*, through which he transferred to this fictional person the credit for the great wisdom and wise counsel of Mr. Franklin. *Poor Richard's Almanac* had a circulation of over ten thousand copies and was by far the most numerous literary piece circulating in the colonies. He also published the *Pennsylvania Gazette*.

As a scientist he founded the "Junto" in 1727. This

word, which comes from a Latin root, means to join. Each of those who became members of this organization determined to become better men. Each agreed to write four articles a year on some uplifting subject matter.

Ben's program for writing out one's thoughts was quite different than the programs of some men to merely dream irresponsibly about their objectives. Ben worked with, and prayed over, and worshipped ideas. About his writing, Ben once said to Miss Read, his future wife, "I have made myself a better printer. Maybe I can make myself a better man if I work at it long enough." Ben absorbed science, philosophy, history, leadership, and self-improvement ideas like a thirsty sponge.

Out of the "Junto" ultimately came the University of Pennsylvania and the American Philosophical Society, which was the forerunner of all of our contemporary scientific organizations. Ben was elected to the Royal Academy, and his observation of ocean currents and atmospheric physics led him to the development of modern meteorology and the discovery of the Gulf Stream. He also invented watertight bulkheads for ships.

Most people have difficulty in developing enough ideas to serve as a basis for their success, but Benjamin Franklin had ideas that just never seemed to cease. He discovered electricity and the lightning rod. He also invented bifocal glasses. He pioneered in street lighting and street cleaning. He founded the first police and fire departments. He invented remedies for smoking chimneys. He discovered how to regulate the speed of barges, and invented a copying machine.

Ben was a co-founder of the Pennsylvania Hospital, and wrote numerous original articles on lead poisoning and common colds. He invented the sun dial and daylight savings time. He took the lead in the organization of a militia force and the paving of the city streets.

He learned to speak French, Spanish, Italian, and Latin. He established the first circulating library. In 1759, for his literary and more particularly his scientific attainments, he received the award of the Freedom of the City of Edinburgh and the degree of Doctor of Law from the University of St. Andrews. He had been made a Master of Arts at Harvard and Yale in 1753 and at the College of William and Mary in 1756. And in 1762, he received a degree of Doctor of Civil Law at Oxford. One of the advantages of learning to think for oneself is that thoughts may be so much more productive when they are self-made. The University of Pennsylvania, which Mr. Franklin established, has never produced anyone to equal him, in spite of the fact that he had only two years of formal schooling in his youth.

Ben was one of the first men to think in terms of the separate colonies as a single entity. He was a director of the postal services, and his efforts to visit the major post offices of the colonies led him to think of them as a unit. He increased the mail service from once a week to three times a week between New York and Philadelphia in the summer. He was eventually elected Post Master General.

His diplomatic service as agent of the colonies before the House of Commons in the 1760's, together with his service as our agent in France, is well known, and represents significant diplomatic achievements. He served as the chief executive officer of the state of Pennsylvania beginning in 1785, and went from there to the Constitutional Convention where he was the oldest member. He also gave the impulse to nearly every measure or project for the welfare and prosperity of Philadelphia undertaken in his day.

In 1751, he became a member of the General Assembly of Pennsylvania in which he served for thirteen years. When war with France seemed imminent in 1754, Franklin was sent to the Albany Convention where he submitted his plan for colonial union. So great was the confidence in Franklin, that early in 1756, the Governor of Pennsylvania placed him in charge of the northwestern frontier of the province with power to raise troops, issue commissions, and erect blockhouses. Franklin remained in the wilderness for a period of time superintending the building of forts and observing the Indians.

While in America, Franklin was accused of being too much of an Englishman. While in England, he was accused of being too much of an American. In Congress, he served simultaneously on as many as ten committees. From July 16 to September 28, 1776, he acted as President of the Constitutional Convention of Pennsylvania.

On September 26, 1776, he was chosen as Commissioner to France. At the time of Franklin's arrival in Paris, he was already one of the most talked about men in the world. He became a member of every important learned society in Europe; he was a member and one of the managers of the Royal Society. Three editions of his scientific works had already appeared in Paris and another edition appeared in London.

Franklin's reputation, wrote John Adams, was more universal than that of Leibnitz or Newton, Frederick or Voltaire, and his character more esteemed and beloved than all of them put together. His service to America in England and France rank him as one of the heroes of the American War of Independence and as the greatest of American diplomats. Almost the only American scientist of his day, he displayed remarkably deep, as well as varied, abilities in science and deserved the honors enthusiastically given to him by the savants of Europe.

If a collection could be made of all of the gazettes of Europe for the latter half of the Eighteenth Century, a greater number of statements praising the *Grand Old Man* (Benjamin Franklin) would not have been found for any other person who had ever lived. "Franklin's appearance in the French salons before he began to negotiate," says Frederick Christoph Schlosser, "was an event of great importance to the whole of Europe. Such was the number of portraits, busts, and medallions of him in circulation before he left Paris that he would have been recognized from them by any adult citizen in any part of the civilized world."

When Franklin was recalled to America in 1785, he was replaced by Thomas Jefferson. When someone asked Jefferson if he was taking the place of Franklin, he replied, "No one can replace him, sir, I am only his successor." Before Franklin left Paris on the 12th of July, 1785, he made commercial treaties with Sweden and Prussia. In May 1787, he was elected a delegate to the convention which drew up the Federal Constitution, this body thus having a member upon whom all could agree as chairman should Washington be absent.

When Franklin's turn came, he stepped forward and signed his name. This was the fourth great document connected with the beginning of the nation, and Franklin was the only man who signed all four; the Declaration of Independence, the Alliance with France, the Treaty with England, and the

Constitution of the United States of America.

He was a great man and a great American. He made the motion that the members of the Constitutional Convention should hold a daily prayer to seek divine guidance for their proceedings. On the back of President Washington's chair there had been emblazoned a half sun. On one occasion when the President was out of his chair so that this figure could be seen, Franklin made a statement saying that in practicing their art, artists have had difficulty in showing whether a half sun was rising or setting. But commenting upon the inspired directions by the members, he said, "Now I have the happiness to know that our sun is a rising sun."

At another time he said, addressing the Chairman of the convention, "I have lived a long time sir, and the longer I live the more convincing proofs I see that God ruleth in the affairs of men." He also said, "Except God shall build the house, we who labor in this convention shall succeed no better than the builders of Babel." Franklin composed a prayer in which he said, "O powerful Goodness! Bountiful Father! Merciful Guide! Increase in me that wisdom which discovers my truest interest. Strengthen my resolution to perform what that wisdom dictates. Accept my kind offices to thy other children, as the only return in my power for thy continual favors to me."

Franklin's work as a publisher was, for the most part, closely connected with his work in issuing the *Gazette and Poor Richard's Almanac*, which is a summary of the many proverbs used by him to stimulate improvement in his readers. Judged as literature, first place belongs to his autobiography which unquestionably still ranks among the few really great autobiographies ever written. Closely related to Franklin's political pamphlets are his writings on economics, which, though undertaken with a political or practical purpose and not in a purely scientific spirit, rank him as the first American economist. His *Way to Wealth*, which was a preface to *Poor Richard's Almanac* in 1758, contains many gems of wisdom, and might serve us as a guide to gaining our own wealth.

Benjamin Franklin was very conscious of the need for personal development. He described a program he designed which, if adapted by us, could prove of great value in broadening our abilities and our moral courage. In 1728, when he was just twenty-two years old, he said, "It was about this time that I conceived the bold and arduous project of arriving at moral perfection. I wished to live without committing any faults at any time. I could conquer all that either natural inclination, custom, or company might lead me into. As I knew or thought I knew what was right and wrong, I did not see why I might not always do the one and avoid the other. But I soon found I had undertaken a task of far more difficulty than I had imagined. While my care was employed in guarding against one fault, I was often surprised by another. Habit took the advantage of inattention. Inclination was sometimes too strong for reason. I concluded at length that the mere speculative conviction that it was to our interest to be completely virtuous was not sufficient to prevent our slipping, and that the contrary habits must be broken and good ones acquired and established before we can have any dependence on a steady, uniform rectitude of conduct. For this purpose, I, therefore, tried the following method."

Benjamin Franklin then wrote down the qualities which he wanted to acquire, with a short precept that expressed the meaning he wished the term to have. Those qualities he listed were:

1. **Temperance**—Eat not to dullness; drink not to elevation.

2. **Silence**—Speak not but what may benefit others or yourself; avoid trifling conversation.

3. **Order**—Let all your things have their places; let each part of your business have its time.

4. **Resolution**—Resolve to perform what you ought; then perform without fail what you resolve.

5. **Frugality**—Make no expense, but to do good to others or yourself; i. e. , waste nothing.

6. **Industry**—Lose no time; be always employed in something useful; cut off all unnecessary actions

7. **Sincerity**—Use no hurtful deceit; think innocently and justly and, if you speak, speak accordingly.

8. **Justice**—Wrong none by doing injuries, or omitting the benefits that are your duty.

9. **Moderation**—Avoid extremes; forbear resenting injuries so much as you think they deserve.

10. **Cleanliness**—Tolerate no uncleanliness in body, clothes, or habitation.

11. **Tranquility**—Be not disturbed at trifles, or at accidents common or unavoidable.

12. **Chastity**—Rarely use venery but for health or offspring, never to dullness, weakness, or the injury of your own or another's peace or reputation.

13. **Humility**—Imitate Jesus and Socrates.

He further said, "My intention being further to acquire the

habit of these virtues, I judged it would be well not to distract my attention by attempting the whole at once, but to fix it on one of them at a time, and when I should be master of that, then to proceed to another and so on until I should have gone through the entire list. I determined to give a week of strict attention to each of the virtues successively, and like him having a garden to weed, does not intend to eradicate all of the bad herbs at once which would exceed his reach and his strength, but works on one of the beds at a time and having accomplished the first proceeds to the second. "

Ben made a small book which he carried with him constantly from the time he was age twenty-two until the time of his death at age eight-four. In this little book he made a check each night of all the places where he had fallen down in his determination to develop these great qualities of personality. After keeping this technique up for fifty-seven years, he made this marvelous statement, "It may be well that my posterity be informed that to this little artifice of constant attention and daily checking on himself, with the blessing of God, their ancestor owed the constant felicity of his life down to his 79th year, in which this is written: 'What reverses may attend the remainder of my life is in the hand of Providence. '"

Building an effective personality wasn't easy for Franklin. He said, "In truth I found myself incorrigible with respect to order, and now I am grown old and my memory's bad, I feel very sensibly the want of it. But on the whole, though I never arrived at the perfection I had been so ambitious to obtain, but fell far short of it, yet I was by the endeavor a better and happier man than I otherwise should have been had I not attempted. "

It is suggested that every one of us should have some

similar means of checking up on himself. Don't be discouraged if your personality doesn't develop to your satisfaction all at once. Remember, Benjamin Franklin worked at it constantly and made a written record of his faults and progress every day for sixty-two years. He gave that one habit a large part of the credit for those things he achieved. The point is that it takes a long time to approach perfection, even if we work at it constantly. Development comes slowly, but with concentrated persistent effort the reward will be richness in life never before imagined.

Probably the most important of those thirteen principles outlined by Franklin was the one of resolution. In explaining what this meant to him, he wrote, "Resolve to perform what you ought, and then perform without fail what you resolve." He said, "Once a resolution becomes a habit, it will keep me firm in my endeavors to obtain all of the subsequent virtues."

Mr. Franklin said he found his habit of sticking to his ambition extremely difficult to acquire. "My faults vexed me so much that I made little progress and had such frequent lapses that I was almost ready to give up the attempt and content myself with a faulty character in that respect." He said, "Like the man who in buying an axe of a smith, desired to have the whole of its surface as bright as the edge, the smith consented to grind the man's axe bright for him if he would turn the wheel. This he did while the smith pressed the broad face of the axe heavily on the stone which made the turning very fatiguing. The man stopped every now and then to see how much progress had been made and at length would take his axe as it was without further grinding. 'No,' said the smith, 'turn on, turn on, we shall have it bright by and by. As yet it is only speckled.' 'Yes,' said the man, 'but I think I liked a speckled axe best. ' And I believe this may be the case with many who, having for want of some such means as I employed, found the difficulty of obtaining good and breaking bad habits, had given up the struggle and concluded that a speckled axe was best after all. "

Death came quietly to Franklin while he was sleeping on April 17, 1790. Congress, which had not yet paid his salary and expenses for his services in France, declared 30 days mourning and joined in the procession to his grave in the cemetery near the Christ Church. The newspapers reported it as the greatest procession ever seen in the city.

Not long after, a bronze plaque was put on the wall by his grave with a statement of his faith in immortality that Ben had written when he was twenty years old and so ill that he thought he would die. It said:

The Body
of B. Franklin
Printer
(Like the cover of an old book
Its contents torn out
And stripped of its lettering and gilding)
Lies here, food for worms.
But the work shall not be lost
For it will (as he believed) appear once more
In a new and more elegant edition
Revised and corrected
by
The Author

MOHANDAS K. GANDHI

A Man of Printicple;
to Believe was to Act.

A number of years ago, Louis Fischer wrote a marvelous book about a great man. It had to do with the life and work of Mohandas K. Gandhi, the Indian patriot, who was largely instrumental in winning the independence of India from England.

Gandhi went around four-fifths naked; he lived in a mud hut that had no electric lights, running water, nor telephone. He didn't own an automobile, and he never sought or ever held a public office. He was without political post, academic distinction, scientific achievement, or artistic gift. He commanded no armies, led no diplomats, and owned no property, yet men with great government and powerful armies behind them paid him homage.

The leaders of the British government soon discovered that England could not rule India against Gandhi and it could not rule India without Gandhi. By the sheer power of his near-naked person, Gandhi raised himself to become the unquestioned leader of 500 million people, and he was as close to being India as anyone or anything could possibly be. He was the greatest power in his country.

With united accord, Gandhi's followers renamed him "The Mahatma," meaning the great soul, and no title could have described him more appropriately. While Gandhi lived among the untouchables, he was a powerful influence in the affairs of two great nations. Louis Fischer calls this phenomenon by which an ordinary human being with meager talents and humble beginnings can raise himself to the heights of great power and accomplishment, "The Miracle of Personality."

Even in our day of astonishing advances, "The Miracle of Personality" is still the most productive of all discoveries. What makes it even more important is that each individual person may perform this important transformation for himself to his own specifications. Personality is the single term used to describe the collection of the individual traits of any particular person.

But no two people are the same. Your personality is your most unique possession, because it distinguishes you from all other people. It comprises those original innate characteristics, as well as whatever else may be added later by education or by life.

Behind the body, the mind, and the behavior, is an invisible reality of spiritual order called the person. The person is what one is at the center. The personality backs up and gives meaning to every other thing in life. No matter how you look at it, personality is the most amazing fact in the universe. All of the powers of memory, reflection, intelligence, ambition, purposefulness, enthusiasm, and love are placed under the command of the personality. Under its influence and domination, we may develop an appreciation of beauty, a love of truth, and an ambition to achieve. It may foretell the possibility of endless accomplishment.

Wealth cannot create personality, but personality can create wealth. Therefore, personality is greater than wealth. Personality cannot be bought. It cannot be inherited. It has no lineal descent and no right of succession. It cannot be delegated or borrowed. No personality accounts are ever transferable. Personality is personally developed and individually used. The value of its individual powers for either good or evil are indicated through this all- important commodity called human life.

Hundreds of years before the birth of Christ, Greek actors wore masks on which was indicated the part that particular actor was to play. This practice enabled the spectators immediately to identify the hero, the villain, and every other actor in the play. The type of mask that each wore ensured that no spectator would be kept waiting to learn the character facts and that no one would make a mistake about the personality of the actors. Later the Romans called these masks "personae. " Even now when we announce the characters in the play, we print the words "Dramatis Personae" on our theater programs. But each individual who takes a part in the play of life creates the mask that he himself will wear.

Gandhi's life started out in the negative. He was burdened down with some rather serious handicaps. He was afraid of the dark; he was afraid of people; he was afraid of himself; and he regarded himself as a coward. In addition, he had some very damaging inferiority complexes as well as an uncontrollable temper.

Realizing the disadvantages that these traits gave him, he deliberately started out to remake himself, and some time before his death at age seventy-eight, he described himself as a "self-made man." For anyone who is looking for a good phrase with startling possibilities, here is one of the best. No performance can be better than the person of the performer.

One of the greatest ambitions of Gandhi's life was to free his country. But he felt that before he could free India from the British, he must free himself from those weaknesses that were holding him down. Gandhi determined to put himself under the perfect control of himself, because more than anything else, he desired to be an effective instrument of negotiation for his country's welfare. How well he succeeded at this goal is known to everyone. It is Mr. Fischer's opinion, that not since Socrates has the world seen Gandhi's equal for effective self-analysis with absolute composure and self-control. By some, he was thought to be the world's most Christ-like person, and yet he was not a Christian.

Gandhi believed in being, not merely in having or in seeming. He believed that the discord between deed and creed lied at the root of innumerable wrongs in his civilization, and that it was the greatest weakness of churches, states, parties, and persons. Gandhi thought that to believe a thing and not to practice it was dishonest, and that this gave institutions and men split personalities. He believed that the personality of every successful man should be well-integrated, properly balanced, and highly motivated.

Gandhi never trifled; he never wavered; he never stumbled into success. He went on long fasts for discipline. He reasoned that if he could not curb his passion for food, how could he handle the more difficult situations in life itself? He said, "How can I control others if I cannot control myself?"

With Gandhi, to believe was to act. There was no

pretense; face-saving was to him an unintelligible concept. When he had decided something was good, he always followed through and translated every helpful thought into an activity. Gandhi realized early in his life that integrity and manhood were among the most important instruments of national and individual power. This gave him great personal advantage in his dealings with others. He said, "I cannot conceive of a greater loss to a man than a loss of his self-respect. "

Even while fighting England for India's independence, Gandhi had the constant respect and trust of the British leaders. He had two mottos which said, "harmony in adversity" and "love despite differences. "

There came a time during the bitter years of World War II when the fate of England was hanging in the balance. England could not spare even a single soldier to fight for the defense of India. Many prominent Indian leaders were in favor of throwing out the oppressive British rule while England was helpless, but Gandhi said no. He said, "We will not steal even our independence. "

Gandhi would have given his life at any moment in exchange for his country's freedom. But he did not want independence if it could not be had honorably. He believed that reason, fairness, and understanding were superior to force as instruments of national negotiation. He always practiced these fundamental principles of right even though he had the power to do as he pleased. Our most sincere compliment to this great and inspiring man might be to say that he was a real person.

By way of contrast, many men living today would not hesitate for an instant to enslave everyone in the world, if only they thought they could. But most of Gandhi's tremendous personal power always remained unused. He said, "We cannot learn discipline by compulsion. " He never retaliated. His reason told him that if the policy of "an eye for an eye" were carried to its ultimate conclusion, it would result in making everybody blind. Gandhi did not attempt to be clever. He once declared, "I have never had recourse to cunning in all of my life. " His mind and emotions were almost as exposed to public view as was his near-naked body.

Gandhi's mother had taught him that eating meat was wrong, inasmuch as it necessitated the destruction of other life. So, young Gandhi made a pledge to his mother that he would remain a strict vegetarian throughout his life. Many years after Gandhi's mother had passed on, Gandhi himself became very ill and was not expected to live. His physicians tried to persuade him that to drink a little beef broth might save his life, but Gandhi said, "Even for life itself, we may not do certain things. There is only one course open to me—to die but never to break my pledge. "

Just imagine what it would mean to our world if all present-day leaders of nations had that kind of integrity. Then every man's word could be absolutely depended upon. Then trust, competence, and mutual respect would be the foundation of every human relationship and every national action. It was in these departments of personal greatness that Gandhi excelled. Everyone understood that Gandhi was absolutely honest, that he could be trusted, and that his motives were pure. When Gandhi said something, everyone knew that was exactly what he meant. Millions trusted Gandhi; millions obeyed him; multitudes counted themselves as his followers; but strangely enough, only a few ever attempted to do as he did. Gandhi's greatness lay in doing what everyone could do, but did not do.

Then came that fateful day, July 30, 1948, at 5:05 p. m. Gandhi was hurrying to the village prayer ground. In the front row of the congregated worshipers sat one Nathuran Godse, clutching a pistol in his pocket. As the two men almost touched each other, Godse fired three bullets into the body of the Mahatma.

In response to Godse's obeisance, Gandhi touched his palms together, smiled, and blessed him. At that moment Godse pulled the trigger, and Gandhi's mortal life came to an end. But even in death, this little brown man was engaged in the act of blessing people and doing good.

A few minutes after Gandhi's death, Prime Minister Nehru went on the radio and said, "The light has gone out of our lives, and there is darkness everywhere, for our beloved leader, the father of our nation, is no more. " At Godse's trial he said he bore no ill will to Gandhi. He said, "Before I fired the shots, I actually wished him well and bowed to him in reverence. "

From the example of Mohandas Gandhi, we might understand what great power can be built up in human lives. We need merely to develop, to their highest denomination, these great God-given qualities with which each of us is endowed.

COLONEL ROBERT G. INGERSOLL

*"Without thoughts,
words are empty purses."*

B orn in Dresden, New York on August 11, 1833, Robert Green Ingersoll was the self- educated son of a congregational minister. He was admitted to practice law before the Illinois Bar in 1854, and he subsequently enjoyed a very lucrative law practice in Peoria, Washington D. C. , and New York City.

Ingersoll rose to the rank of Colonel during the Civil War, where he served as a member of the Illinois Volunteer Cavalry. This title he used and enjoyed all the rest of his life. His war service was terminated in 1862, when he was captured and subsequently paroled by Confederate General Nathan Bedford Forrest.

As an orthodox Republican, Ingersoll was elected Attorney General of Illinois, and served in that position from 1867 to 1869. He was described as the "Big Voice" of the Republican Party in the presidential campaigns of 1876 and 1880. In spite of his contributions to the Party as a speaker, his controversial religious views deterred Republican administration leaders from appointing him to the Cabinet or other high diplomatic posts.

He was nationally known as a lecturer. He was in great demand and received as much as $3,500 for a single evening's performance, which in those days was a tremendous amount. The writings of Robert G. Ingersoll were published in twelve volumes in 1902 and were edited by Clinton B. Ferrell. A biography of his life was also written in 1952 by C. H. Cramer, which was entitled *Royal Bob*.

I have had the very pleasant experience of reading the complete works of Robert G. Ingersoll, made up of some 19,900 pages. I did not skip read or fast read or select from among the total. I took each page, one at a time, and tried to understand what was written there before I turned to the next. I have felt a little bit cheated in my life that no one has ever tried to talk me out of my faith, and I have felt some times that maybe I believed as I did because I didn't understand the opposite point of view. Because Robert G. Ingersoll served as America's leader in this thing we call "higher criticism of the Bible," I chose him for the one to test my faith upon.

I am pleased to report that, in my opinion, I passed the test and came out of this reading experience with a large profit. Whatever might be said about his lack of religious conviction, he certainly was a great architect of speech. He knew how to put language together. He knew how to make ideas memorable and impressive. Above everything else, to me, he represented oratory and powerful, effective speech. He committed his speeches to memory although they were sometimes more than three hours long. His audiences were said never to be restless.

It has been said that oratory is the process of dressing

language up in its best clothes and giving it a maximum of meaning and power. An oration is an elaborate discourse, treating an important subject impressively. An orator is an artist with words. He knows how to measure, color, and weigh speech in order to give it its greatest possible fire-power.

An orator has been described as one who knows how to think on his feet. He has a passion for expression, a face that thought illuminates, and a voice that is harmonious with the ideas expressed. An orator has logic like a column, and poetry like a vine. He transforms the commonplace, and dresses his ideas up in purple and fine linen. In a dozen different ways, he creates the climate in which the best ambitions of people flourish and burst into full bloom.

Many of the great events of our history remain in our minds, not because of the thing itself, but because someone has effectively told about it. We remember Paul Revere's ride because Longfellow set the galloping hooves of the steed to the music of impressive speech. Other riders may have done a greater service than Paul Revere, but they have not lived on in history because they had no one to impressively recite their deeds.

At the national political convention held on June 16, 1876, Colonel Ingersoll was selected to nominate James C. Blaine as a candidate for President of the United States. The press told of the great prestige that Colonel Ingersoll had among the people, and described the effect that he had upon this particular audience by saying,

> Ingersoll moved out from an obscure corner and advanced to the central stage. As he walked forward, he was greeted with thundering cheers.

As he reached the platform, the cheers took on an increased volume and for ten minutes the surging fury of acclamation, the wild waving of fans, hats, and handkerchiefs transformed the scene from one of deliberation to that of a bedlam of rapturous delirium.

Ingersoll waited with unimpaired serenity, until he could get a chance to be heard . . . and then he began his impassioned, artful, brilliant, and persuasive appeal.

Possessed with a fine figure, and a face of winning cordial frankness, Ingersoll had half won his audience before he spoke a word. And it was the attestation of every man who heard him, that such a brilliant master- stroke had never before been uttered before a political convention. Its effect was indescribable. The coolest heads in the hall were stirred to the wildest expression.

The adversaries of Blaine, as well as his friends, listened with unswerving, absorbed attention. Curtis sat spellbound, his eyes and mouth were wide open, his figure moving in unison to the tremendous periods that fell in a measured exquisitely graduated flow from Ingersoll's smiling lips.

The matchless method and manner of this man can never be understood from any report in type. To realize the prodigious force, the inexpressible power, the irrestrainable fervor of his audience requires actual sight. Words can do but meager justice to the magic power of this extraordinary man. He swayed and moved and impelled and restrained the mass before him as if he possessed a magic key to that innermost mechanism that moves the human heart. When he finished, his fine, frank face was as calm as when he began, and the overwrought thousands sank back in an exhaustion of unspeakable wonder and delight.

As has been said, it is very difficult to describe power and effectiveness in speech. It must be heard and felt. And while Colonel Ingersoll is not now available for a demonstration, he has left many volumes of his words in print.

The second best way to understand may be to read what he said and imagine how his influence might have made us feel. An oration is related to an oratorio, and an oratorio is a dramatic text or poem usually founded on a scriptural theme and set to music.

A large number of our present-day problems have come about because so many of our communication skills have been lost in recent years. We seem unable to talk effectively any more. If we try to follow the orators, we may be afraid of an accusation of affectation. Frequently we do not want to be that deeply involved with life, and so we drop our more intense feelings and convictions and settle back into the greater comforts of the ordinary.

We can draw some of the emotion and music and rhythm of an oratorio by listening to it. And we can feel some of the elegance and power of Colonel Ingersoll's expression by reading his words and feeling their power. For example, he once made the following denunciation of booze which then, as now, is one of our most serious public enemies. Colonel

Ingersoll said,

> Everyone who touches whiskey is demoralized. It demoralizes those who make it, those who sell it, and those who drink it, from the time it issues from the coiled and poisonous worm of the distillery, until it empties into the hell of crime, dishonor and death, it demoralizes everyone who comes in contact with it.
>
> I do not believe that anyone can contemplate the subject without becoming prejudiced against this stream of death, including the suicides, the insanities, the poverty, the ignorance, the distress of the little children tugging at the faded dresses of weeping and despairing wives asking for bread, the men of genius it has ruined, of the millions struggling with imaginary serpents produced by this devilish thing. And when you think of the jails, of the almshouses, of the asylums, of the prisons, of the scaffolds, I do not wonder that every thoughtful man is prejudiced against the damned stuff called alcohol.

Colonel Ingersoll effectively expressed himself on a great many other subjects, as recorded in the 19,900 pages of his works. In one of his greatest statements, he told about a visit to the tomb of Napoleon and what he thought about it. This is one of the most effective uses of words with which I am familiar. It is reproduced in the chapter entitled, "Napoleon the Great."

Two of the funeral orations of Colonel Ingersoll

are included herewith. One was given at a child's grave at Washington, D. C. , on January 8, 1882, as follows:

My friends: I know how vain it is to gild a grief with words, and yet I wish to take from every grave its fear. Here in this world, where life and death are equal kings, all should be brave enough to meet that which all the dead have met. The future has been filled with fear, stained and polluted by a heartless past. From the wondrous tree of life the buds and blossoms fall with ripened fruit, and in the common bed of earth, patriarchs and babes sleep side by side.

Why should we fear that which will come at last to all that is? We cannot tell, we do not know, which is the greater blessing–life or death. We cannot say that death is not a good thing. We do not know whether the grave is the end of this life, or the door of another, or whether the night here is not somewhere else a dawn. Neither can we tell which is the more fortunate; the child dying in its mother's arms, before its lips have learned to form a word, or he who journeys all the length of life's uneven road, painfully taking the last slow steps with staff and crutch.

Every cradle asks us 'Whence?' and every coffin 'Whither?' The poor barbarian, weeping above his dead, can answer these questions just as well as the robed priest of the most authentic creed. The tearful ignorance of the one is as consoling as the learned and unmeaning words of the other. No man, standing where the horizon of a life has touched a grave, has any right to prophesy a future filled with pain and tears.

It may be that death gives all there is of worth to life. If those we press and strain within our arms could never die, perhaps that love would wither from the earth. Maybe this common fate treads from out the paths between our hearts the weeds of selfishness and hate. And I had rather live and love where death is king, than have eternal life where love is not. Another life is naught, unless we know and love again the ones who love us here.

They, who stand with breaking hearts around this little grave, need have no fear. The larger and the nobler faith in all that is, and is to be, tells us that death, even at its worst, is only perfect rest. We know that through the common wants of life—the needs and duties of each hour—their grief will lessen day by day, until at last this grave will be to them a place of rest and peace—almost of joy. There is for them this consolation—the dead do not suffer. If they live again, their lives will surely be as good as ours. We have no fear. We are all children of the same mother, and the same fate awaits us all. We, too, have our religion, and it is this: Help for the living—hope for the dead.

Colonel Ingersoll had made an agreement with his brother, Eldon, that whoever died first the other would give the eulogy at his funeral. On the occasion of his brother's funeral, Colonel Ingersoll said:

Dear Friends: I am going to do that which the dead oft promised he would do for me.

The loved and loving brother, husband, father, friend, died where manhood's morning almost touches noon, and while the shadows still were falling toward the west.

He had not passed on life's highway the stone that marks the highest point; but being weary for a moment, he lay down by the wayside, and using his burden for a pillow, fell into that dreamless sleep that kisses down his eyelids still. While yet in love with life and raptured with the world, he passed to silence and pathetic dust.

Yet after all, it may be best, just in the happiest, sunniest hour of all the voyage, while eager winds are kissing every sail, to dash against the unseen rock, and in an instant hear the billows roar above a sunken ship. For whether in mid sea or among the breakers of the farther shore, a wreck at last must mark the end of each and all. And every life, no matter if its every hour is rich with love and every moment jeweled with a joy, will at its close, become a tragedy as sad and deep and dark as can be woven of the warp and woof of mystery and death.

This brave and tender man in every storm of life was oak and rock; but in the sunshine he was vine and flower. He was the friend of all heroic souls. He climbed the heights, and left all superstitions far below, while on his forehead fell the golden dawning of the grander day.

He loved the beautiful, and was with color,

form, and music touched to tears. He sided with the weak, the poor, the wronged, and lovingly gave alms. With loyal heart and with purest hands he faithfully discharged all public trusts.

He was a worshipper of liberty, a friend of the oppressed. A thousand times I have heard him say these words: 'For justice all places a temple, and all seasons, summer.' He believed that happiness was the only good, reason the only torch, justice the only worship, humanity the only religion, and love the only priest. He added to the sum of human joy; and were every one to whom he did some loving service to bring a blossom to his grave, he would sleep tonight beneath a wilderness of flowers.

Life is a narrow vale between the cold and the barren peaks of two eternities. We strive in vain to look beyond the heights. We cry aloud, and the only answer is the echo of our wailing cry. From the voiceless lips of the unreplying dead there comes no word; but in the night of death hope sees a star and listening love can hear the rustle of a wing.

He who sleeps here, when dying, mistaking the approach of death for the return of health, whispered with his latest breath, 'I am better now.' Let us believe, in spite of doubts and dogmas, of fears and tears, that these dear words are true of all the countless dead.

The record of a generous life runs like a vine around the many men he loved, to do the last sad office for the dead, we give his sacred dust. Speech cannot contain our love. There was, there is, no gentler, stronger, manlier man.

A reporter of the New York Sun once asked Colonel Ingersoll, "What advice would you give to a young man who was ambitious to become a successful orator?" And under the date of April, 1896, the Sun published Colonel Ingersoll's reply under the title of "How to Become an Orator," from which everyone might profit, whether he ever expects to make a public speech or not. In substance, Colonel Ingersoll said:

In the first place I would advise him to have something to say that is worth saying and that people will be glad to hear. Behind of the art of speaking must be the power to think. Without thoughts, words are empty purses. Most people imagine that almost any words uttered in a loud voice and accompanied by appropriate gestures, constitute an oration.

I would advise the young man to study his subject, to find what others had thought, to look at it from all sides. Then I would tell him to write out his thoughts or to arrange them in his mind, so that he would know exactly what he was going to say. Waste no time on the 'how' until you are satisfied with the 'what.'

After you know what you are going to say, then you can think about how it should be said. Then you can think about the tone, emphasis, and gestures. But if you really understand and believe what you say, emphasis, tone, and gesture will more or less take care of themselves. All of these should come from inside so that the thought will be in perfect harmony with the feelings. Voice and gesture should be governed by strong emotions. The orator must be true to his subject, and avoid any references to himself.

The great column of his argument should go unbroken. He can adorn it with vines and flowers, but not in such profusion that they hide the column. He should give it the variety of episode by illustrations for the purpose of adding strength to the argument.

The man who wishes to become an orator should study language. He should know the deeper meanings of words. He should understand the vigor and velocity of verbs and the color of adjectives. He should know how to sketch a scene and so paint a picture with words and feeling that it is given life and action. A perfect picture requires lights and shadows, and now and then a flash of lightning may illuminate the intellectual sky. He should be a poet and a dramatist, a painter and an actor. He should cultivate his imagination. He should become familiar with the great poetry and fiction that is so rich in heroic deeds. He should be a student of Shakespeare. He should read and devour the great plays and should learn the art of expression and comprehension with all of the secrets of the head and the heart.

The great orator is full of variety and surprises. His speech is a panorama. The interest does not flag. He does not allow himself to be anticipated. He does not repeat himself. A picture is shown but once. An orator should avoid the commonplace. He should put no cotton with his silk, no common metals with his gold. He should remember that 'gilded dust is not as good as dusted gold.'

The great orator is honest, and sincere, he does not pretend. His brain and heart work together. Nothing is forced. And every drop of his blood is convinced. He knows exactly what he wishes to say . . . and stops when he has finished.

Only a great orator knows when and how to close. Most speakers go on after they are through. They are satisfied with a 'lame and impotent conclusion.' Most speakers lack variety. They travel a dusty road, whereas the great orator convinces and charms by indirection.

Of course, no one can tell another what to do to become an orator, I can tell him a few things not to do. There should be no introduction to an oration. The orator should commence with his subject. There should be no prelude, no flourish, no apology, and no explanation. He should say nothing about himself.

Like a sculptor, he stands by his block of stone. Every stroke is for a purpose and its form soon begins to appear. When the statue is finished the workman stops. Nothing is more difficult than a perfect close. Few poems, few pieces of music or novels end well. A good story, a great speech, a perfect poem, should all end just at the proper point. Thoughts are not born of chance. They grow, bud, blossom, and bear the fruit of perfect form. Genius is the climate, but the soil must be cultivated and the harvest does not come immediately after the planting. It takes time and labor to raise a crop from that field called the brain.

Colonel Ingersoll went on to mention some other great orators. He said:

Theodore Parker was an orator. He preached great sermons. His sermons on 'Old Age' and 'Webster' and his address on 'Liberty' were filled with great thoughts, marvelously expressed. When he dealt with human events, with realities, with the things he knew, then he was superb. When he spoke of freedom, of duty, of living to the ideal, of mental integrity, he seemed inspired.

Webster had the great qualities of force, dignity, clearness and grandeur. Clay had a commanding presence, a noble bearing, a heroic voice. He was a natural leader, a wonderful, forcible, persuasive, convincing talker. He was not a poet, nor a master of metaphor, but he was practical. He kept in view the end to be accomplished. He was the opposite of Webster. Clay was the morning, Webster the evening. Clay had large views, and a wide horizon. He was ample, vigorous, and a little tyrannical.

S. S. Prentiss was an orator. He said profound and beautiful things and uttered the most sublime thoughts.

In my judgment, Corwin was the greatest orator of them all. He had many arrows in his quiver.

He had genius. He was full of humor, pathos, wit, and logic. He was an actor, his body talked. His meaning was in his eyes as well as on his lips. Governor Morton of Indiana had the greatest power of statement that I have ever heard. His facts were perfectly sound and his conclusion was a necessity.

Lincoln had reason, wonderful humor, and wit. But his presence was not good. His voice was poor, his gestures awkward. But his thoughts were profound–his speech at Gettysburg is one of the masterpieces of the world.

Of course, I have heard a great many talkers, but orators are few and far between. They are produced by victorious nations, born in the midst of great events and marvelous achievements. They utter the thoughts, the aspirations of their age. They clothe people in the gorgeous robes of genius. They interpret dreams, and with the poets they prophesize. They fill the future with heroic forms and lofty deeds. They keep their faces toward the dawn of the ever-coming day.

When Alexander the Great finished the job of conquering the world, he wanted to be an orator like his teacher, Aristotle. And Aristotle agreed to teach him. Accordingly, Aristotle wrote out and published his sixteen laws of oratory. Alexander was very disturbed when he returned from a military campaign and discovered that Aristotle had published the laws of oratory and sent them all over Macedonia. The secret was out, and he said to his teacher, "Alas, now everyone will become an orator."

And that would probably be true if everyone were to work on the laws of effective speech as conscientiously as did Aristotle. However, what the great Alexander did not know was that even the greatest men publish their most prized secrets of success, but few people will make any serious attempt to follow them.

Our day is one of great confusion, and it may be that we could solve many of our problems by an increased skill in communications. We live in the most wonderful age in history, and our ability in expression should match our opportunities for expression.

JOAN OF ARC

*"I will not look back
to see if anyone else is following."*

When we love a noble quality in another person, we often tend to embody it in ourselves. The quality of embodied love in others enables us to see this great trait with our eyes and hear it with our ears and treasure it more effectively in our hearts.

I recently felt some very pleasing emotions as I read an account of the life of Joan of Arc. It was written by Sier Louis de Conte, who was born in the same village as she, and was constantly by her side as her page and secretary during her long war. An account of her life was also published in two volumes, by Mark Twain under the title of *Personal Recollections of Joan of Arc*. In all the annals of our time, Joan's life stands out as one of the most striking embodiments of goodness, nobility, and greatness. I believe it is profitable for us to be associated with a personal history of her short but useful career.

Her biography itself is unique. It was written in court and comes to us under oath from the witness stand. It was taken from the official records of the great trial held in the year

1431 at which she was condemned to be burned alive. Every intimate detail of her short and colorful life is still preserved in the National Historical Archives of France.

Joan of Arc was born in the little village of Domremy, France, in 1412. Throughout her childhood, she was extraordinarily healthy and happy. She was wholehearted in her play. Her merry disposition was supplemented by a warm, sympathetic nature. She had frank, winning ways, was genuinely religious, and was greatly admired and loved by everyone.

During this period, France was suffering the cruel pains of its Hundred Years' War with England. France had lost almost every battle. Eight thousand Englishmen had wiped out sixty thousand Frenchmen at Agincourt. French courage had been paralyzed, and France had been reduced to little more than a British province. For Joan, who carried France upon her heart, the continual atrocities of war greatly sobered her spirit and frequently reduced her to tears. Then, in her thirteenth year, Joan began to hear voices, telling her that she would be God's instrument in setting France free.

Among her instructors were Saint Margaret and Saint Catherine. Three years were required to prepare her for her mission. At first she had offered objections. She said to her instructors, "But I am so young to leave my home and mother. How can I talk with men and be a comrade of soldiers? I am only a girl and know nothing of war or even how to ride a horse. How can I lead armies?" Her voice was often broken with sobs, but finally she accepted her call and said, "If it is commanded, I will go. I know that France will rise again, for God has ordained her to be free."

Her voices told her to go to the Governor of

Vaucouleurs who would provide her with an escort of men-at-arms and send her to the Dauphin, who was the uncrowned heir to the throne. In leaving her village home Joan said, "I am enlisted. God helping me, I will not turn back until the British grip is loosened from the throat of France." When the governor had heard her message he said, "What nonsense is this? You are but a child." But Joan said, "Nevertheless, I am appointed by the King of Heaven to lead the armies of France to raise the British siege of Orleans and crown the Dauphin at Rheims."

When the news reached the Dauphin that an unlearned seventeen-year-old peasant maid was coming to see him with a divine commission to free France, he appointed a committee of court advisors to hear her message. Confronting the committee she said, "Forgive me, reverend sirs, but I have no message save for the ears of his Grace, the Dauphin." Their arguments and threats were useless.

After they had left in great anger, she said to her friends, "My mission is to move the Dauphin by argument and reasoning to give me men-at-arms and send me to the siege. Even if the committee carried the message in the exact words with no word missing, and yet left out the persuasions of gesture, the supplicating tone and beseeching looks that inform the words and make them live, then where was the value of that argument and whom could it convince?"

This untaught child had just discarded her shepherd's crook, and yet she was able to penetrate the cunning devices of trained men and defeat them at their own game. She would soon stand unafraid before nobles and other mighty men; she was fully prepared to clothe herself in steel and become the deliverer of France.

When she finally gained an audience with him, the Dauphin said to her, "Tell me who you are." Joan said, "I am called Joan the Maid. I am sent to say to you that the king of heaven wills that you should give me men-at-arms and set me at my appointed work. For I will raise the siege of Orleans and break the British power." But how could she win victories for France where the nation's best-trained generals had had nothing but defeats for over fifty years? But Joan had said that "When God fights, it is a small matter whether the hand that holds the sword is big or little."

This unlearned girl said to the Dauphin, "Be not afraid, God has sent me to save you." Everyone knew that in her heart there was something that raised her above the greatest men of her day. Whether she was come of God or not, they could feel that mysterious something that was later to put heart into her soldiers and turn mobs of cowards into armies of fighters. Her men forgot what fear was when they were in her presence. Her soldiers went into battle with joy in their eyes and a song on their lips. They swept over the battlefield like an irresistible storm. The Dauphin knew that that was the only spirit that could save France, come from whence it may.

Joan won the confidence of the Dauphin and the court with her sweetness, simplicity, sincerity, and unconscious eloquence. The best and the most capable among them recognized that she was formed on a grander plan and moved on a loftier plane than the ordinary mass of mankind. And whence could come such sublime courage and conviction but from God himself?

Finally Joan was given her command. In a public proclamation the Dauphin said, "Know all men, that the most illustrious Charles, by the grace of God, King of France, is pleased to confer upon this well-beloved servant, Joan of Arc, called the Maid, the title, emoluments, and authorities of General-in-Chief of the armies of France. ''

A suit of armor was made for her at Tours. It was of the finest steel, heavily plated with silver, richly ornamented with the engraved designs and polished like a mirror. She was miraculously provided with a sacred sword long hidden behind the alter of St. Catherine's at Fierbois. She herself designed and consecrated a banner which she always carried with her into battle.

As the war march of Joan of Arc began, the curtain went up on one of the most unusual of all military careers. Louis Kossuth said that "Since the writing of human history began, Joan of Arc is the only person of either sex who has ever held supreme command of the military forces of a great nation at age seventeen." She rode a white horse and carried in her hand the sacred sword of Fierbois. It was also the symbol of her authority and the righteousness which she always maintained. She once said to her generals that even the rude business of war could be better conducted without profanity or any of the other brutalities of speech, "

Some could not understand why Joan continued to be alert, vigorous, and confident while her strongest men were exhausted by heavy marches and exposure. They might have reflected that a great soul with a great purpose can make a weak body strong and able to bear the most exhausting fatigues.

Once with an almost impossible objective ahead, Joan said to one of her generals, "I will lead the men over the wall." The general replied, "Not a man will follow you." Joan said, "I will not look back to see whether anyone is following or not."

But the soldiers of France did follow Joan of Arc. With her sacred sword, her consecrated banner, and her belief in her mission, she swept all before her. She sent a thrill of courage and enthusiasm through the French army such as neither king nor generals could produce. Then on May the 8th, 1430, by sheer strategy and force, she broke the siege at Orleans. This anniversary is still celebrated in France as "Joan of Arc Day. " It is the day that she drove out the British and saved France. Then at the head of her troops she marched to Rheims and crowned the Dauphin King.

With her mission accomplished, Joan planned to return to her family in Domremy, but she was treacherously betrayed and sold to the British. Then her long trial of over a year began. For many weary months she was kept in chains. She was threatened and abused. The judges and jurors were carefully selected enemies. Trumped- up charges of witchcraft and sorcery were brought against her. No one doubted that she had seen and conversed with supernatural beings. She had spoken prophecies and had done many things that could not be explained otherwise.

But her enemies argued that her success came from Satan rather than God, and therefore she must be destroyed. Church influence and civil power were both used to discredit her. She was promised her freedom if she would deny her voices and her mission. But Joan was immovable. She said, "If I were under sentence and saw the fire before me or even if I were in flames themselves I would not say other than what I have said at these trials, and I will abide by my testimony until I die. "

A full year had now passed since she had gone speeding across the plain at the head of her troops, her silver helmet shining, her silvery cape fluttering in the wind, her white plumes flowing and her sword held aloft. But Joan of Arc would ride no more. And as the fires were being lighted around the stake at which this nineteen-year-old French peasant maid would be burned alive, she was again given a chance to regain her liberty by denying what she believed.

In choosing the fire above her freedom, she said, "The world can use these words. I know this now–every man gives his life for what he believes; every woman gives her life for what she believes." Sometimes people believe in little or nothing, and yet they give their lives to that little or nothing. One life is all we have, and we live it as we believe in living it and then it is gone. But to surrender what you are, and live without belief, is more terrible than dying, even more terrible than dying young.

Twenty-four years after her death, the Pope appointed a commission to examine the facts of Joan's life, and award a judgment. The commission sat at Paris, at Domrey, at Rouen, and at Orleans. It worked for several months and reinvestigated every detail of her life. It examined the trial records and hundreds of personal witnesses. And through all of this exhaustive examination, Joan's character remained as spotless as it had always been.

Someone said that for "all of the qualities that men call great, look for them in Joan of Arc, and there you will find them." As a result of the Pope's official investigation, Joan of Arc was canonized a saint. The greatest praise was placed upon the official record of her life, there to remain forever.

It has been said that Joan of Arc lived in the most brutal, wicked, and rotten age since the Dark Ages. But Joan was truthful, when lying was the common speech of man. She was honest, when honesty was a lost virtue. She maintained her personal dignity, unimpaired in an age of fawnings and servilities.

She had dauntless courage when hope had perished in the hearts of her countrymen. She was spotlessly pure in mind and body when most of society was foul in both. In nineteen short years, this untaught girl had become the deliverer of France, the savior of her country. She was the genius of patriotism and the embodiment of sainthood, with a martyr's crown upon her head. Joan of Arc was all of these things when crime was the common business of mankind.

Joan of Arc was, perhaps, the only entirely unselfish person whose name has held a high place in profane history. No vestige or suggestion of self-seeking can be found in any word or deed of hers. When she rescued her king and set the crown upon his head, she was offered many rewards and honors, but she refused them all. Although she was the companion of princes, the general of victorious armies, and the idol of an applauding and grateful nation, yet all she desired was to go back to her village and tend her sheep, and to feel her mother's arms about her.

The work of Joan of Arc may fairly be regarded as ranking among the greatest in history. She found a great nation lying in chains, helpless and hopeless under an alien conqueror, its treasury bankrupt, its soldiers disheartened, its king cowed and preparing to flee the country. But when she laid her hand upon this withered nation, its people arose and followed her. Her soul was the embodiment of nobility and righteousness. And it was said that she was the loveliest and the most adorable embodiment of good that any age has yet produced.

ABRAHAM LINCOLN

"The things I want to know are in books . . ."

As Abraham Lincoln lay upon his death bed, Edmund Stanton, his great Secretary of War, looked down upon the lifeless form of the martyred President and said, "Now he belongs to the ages. " This is a truth that has a great literal value for us and our times. Not only did Lincoln cleanse our land of the blight of human slavery and bequeath to us a united nation, but his sense of right and wrong, his moral courage, his patience, integrity, and spirituality were also bequeathed to us.

On Sunday, April 23, 1865, as Lincoln lay in state at Independence Hall in Philadelphia, Phillip Brooks preached a memorial sermon in his honor. He pointed out that the body of Lincoln at that moment rested upon the very spot where four years earlier Lincoln had stood and said, "I would rather be assassinated than give up the principles embodied in the Declaration of Independence. " Lincoln lived as he did because he was what he *was*, and what he was may *now* also belong to us.

As Jesus was concluding His earthly ministry He said to His chief apostle, "Feed my sheep. " Lincoln attempted and succeeded in fulfilling this commandment in a very interesting and constructive way; he fed hungry souls with sympathy and kindness. He set the table of his own example, as a consequence of which we may feast upon fairness, patriotism, and a sense of duty which will make any nation or any individual grow strong and vigorous.

Lincoln taught the world the sacredness of government, the wickedness of man's inhumanity to man, and the value of human dignity and honor. To look up to him even now makes our souls glad and invigorates them with his love of liberty and righteousness. More than almost anyone else who ever lived, he knew how to love truth and yet be charitable, how to hate wrong and oppression, but carry no malice.

Abraham Lincoln loved all men from the highest and most privileged to the lowest and most enslaved. He fed mankind with a reverent and genuine spirituality and a love of God which would work miracles in serving our present need. To the last he reached out a generous hand to feed the South with mercy, the North with charity, and the whole land with peace and happiness.

Then when Lincoln's work was done he suffered a martyr's death. Jesus, gave His life for the world, Lincoln gave his life for his country. We might well devote ourselves to a more earnest contemplation of his great character traits and those eternal principles which he helped to establish in our national code of honor and which are also made available for our own lives. In his example, we can find the solutions for many of the vexing problems of our own day.

Lincoln's birthplace was one of comparable lowliness

with Him who had been born in a Bethlehem stable. Thomas Lincoln and Nancy Hanks, two uneducated farmers, became the parents of a baby boy born on February 12, 1809 in a one room log cabin in Kentucky. Often described as having been born under hopeless conditions, Abraham Lincoln seemed destined to become great.

From her own deathbed, Nancy Hanks Lincoln said to her nine-year-old son, "Abe, go out there and amount to something." And Abe did just that! Later in his life Lincoln said, "All that I am or ever hope to be, I owe to my angel mother." After her death, Abe helped his father put together the rough box that served as her casket. We can picture this little broken-hearted boy as he sat weeping at his mother's bed. However, there was not much time for tears, and Abe bravely trudged a hundred miles to help arrange a Christian burial for his mother.

Suppose, that in our imagination, we follow Abe as he grew to manhood amid difficult conditions. Henry Watterson summed up Lincoln's lack of opportunities by saying, "No teachers, no books, no charts except his own untutored mind. No compass except his own undisciplined will. No light save the light from heaven. Yet like the story of Columbus, he struggles on and on and on toward an unknown destiny."

As a boy and as a man he lived the hard, needy life of a frontiersman, fully responsible for his own needs. We see him emerge from these vigorous experiences as a full-grown man with great moral convictions and solid intellectual opinions. A neighbor once said of him, "He can sink an axe deeper into wood than any man I ever knew."

Physical conditions should never be forgotten in making up one's character. The strength, the muscular activity, and the power of doing and enduring in Lincoln's hard- living ancestors, was appropriated for his own use through discipline of bodily toil. His mind and spirit grew as robust as his body, and all were blended together in such a way that none of them could be considered alone. He avoided hunting and fishing because he did not like killing animals even for food and, though unusually tall and strong, spent so much time reading that some neighbors suspected he must be doing it to avoid strenuous manual labor.

Lincoln's formal education amounted to less than two years, but throughout his life he made the most of every learning opportunity. He mastered the Bible, William Shakespeare's works, English history and American history, and developed a plain writing style that puzzled audiences more accustomed to lofty rhetoric. At noon- time he would sit down under a tree to eat his lunch and at the same time feed his mind from books. His studies were continued at night before the open fire. He said, "I will prepare now and take my chances when the opportunity arrives." He also said, "The things I want to know are in books, and my best friend is the one who will get me a book I haven't read."

Abe's two favorite books were the *Holy Bible* and *The Life of Washington* by Mason R. Weems. These books helped to light the lamps in the dark rooms of his backwoods existence. On one occasion, he left the book *The Life of Washington* out in the rain. Then he confessed his negligence to Josiah Crawford who had loaned him the book and he pulled fodder for three days in payment.

Books seemed to tell young Abe more than they told other boys, and one of his unusual talents was his ability to put what he learned in force. For example, Lincoln refused to join some boyhood friends in lighting a fire on the back of a live mud turtle. Then he wrote a paper arguing against cruelty to animals.

Soon stories began going around about Lincoln's learning, morality, and honesty. He walked six miles to pay back a few cents a woman had overpaid for dry goods. Carl Sandburg said, "He drank enough whiskey only to learn that it was not good for his mind or body. He smoked enough tobacco only to find out that he didn't want to be a smoker."

Someone told him of a book on grammar that John C. Vance had in his house six miles away. He walked the six miles, brought the book back, and burned pine shavings to read it by. Lincoln soon developed strong convictions about education, books, religion, and morality. "In him was combined the greatness of real goodness and the goodness of real greatness." The twain became as one flesh in him. It was about a fifty-fifty guess whether his wise judgments came mostly from a level head or a strong heart. In him goodness and intelligence combined to make him what he was. Real success consists not only in having the right character ingredients, but they must also be put together in the right combinations and proportions.

One admirable side of Lincoln's character is revealed by the fact that he kept two of his most bitter enemies in his cabinet because he wanted their frank criticisms and honest suggestions. How different from some of the selfish, godless tyrants who put millions of people to death because of the slightest suspicion of disagreement. How fortunate that there have been no American Joseph Stalins who were downgraded in a public exhibition of posthumous humiliation by ejecting their mortal remains to occupy some less honorable location because of the mass murders or enslavement of millions of their own people.

What a different kind of spirit we have in the life of Lincoln. He said, "I have always thought that all men should be free, but if any should be slaves, it should be first those who desire it for themselves, and secondly, those who desire it for others. Whenever I hear anyone arguing for slavery, I feel a strong impulse to see it tried on him personally."

Lincoln said, "If human slavery is not wrong, then nothing is wrong. As I would not be a slave, so I would not be a master. Destroy the spirit of liberty, and you have planted the seeds of despotism at your own doors. Familiarize yourselves with the chains of bondage and you prepare your own limbs to wear them. When you have accustomed yourself to trample upon the rights of others, you have lost the genius of your own independence." He declared with integrity and deep conviction, "It is difficult to make a man miserable while he feels he is worthy of himself and claims kinship to the great God who made him." Lincoln added passionately, "I shall try to correct errors when they are shown to be errors, and I shall adopt new views so fast as they shall appear to be true views, and I intend no modification of my oft-expressed personal wish that all men everywhere should be free."

How different from the announced communist objective to enslave everyone in the world. How fortunate for us that we had Washington and Lincoln presiding in the critical periods of our history rather than someone like Stalin or Khrushchev. With a different kind of man in office during our Revolutionary or Civil War periods, our history might have been quite different.

On March 4, 1865, in his second inaugural address,

we too can feel the real heartbeat of Lincoln as he said:

> Each party looked for an easier triumph, and a result less fundamental and astounding. Both read the same Bible and pray to the same God; and each invokes his aid against the other. It may seem strange that any men should dare to ask a just God's assistance in wringing their bread from the sweat of other men's faces; but let us judge not that we be not judged.
>
> The prayers of both could not be answered; that of neither has been answered fully. The Almighty has His own purposes. Woe unto the world because of offences! For it must needs be that offences come; but woe to that man by whom they cometh.
>
> If we shall suppose that American slavery is one of those offences which, in the providence of God, must needs come, and that He gives to both North and South, this terrible war, as the woe due to those by whom the offence came, shall we discern therein any departure from those divine attributes which the believers in a living God always ascribe to Him? Fondly do we hope—fervently do we pray—that this mighty scourge of war may speedily pass away. Yet, if God wills that it continue until all the wealth piled by the bondman's two hundred and fifty years of unrequited toil shall be sunk, and until every drop of blood drawn with the lash shall be paid by another drawn with the sword, as was said three thousand years ago, so still it must be said, 'the judgments of the Lord are true and righteous altogether.'

With malice toward none; with charity for all; with firmness in the right, as God, gives us to see the right, let us strive on to finish the work we are in; to bind up the nation's wounds; to care for him who shall have borne the battle, and for his widow, and his orphan—to do all which may achieve and cherish a just, and a lasting peace, among ourselves, and with all nations.

On the anniversary of Lincoln's birth, and each and every day of the year, we may well strive to get the message of his life into our own hearts for our edification and profit.

MADAME CURIE

"I will not cease to work for it as long as I live."

One of the most inspiring women of our time, and one of our civilization's greatest benefactors, was Marie Sklodowska. She was born in Warsaw, Poland, in 1867. Later she moved to Paris and married Pierre Curie, the French chemist and physicist. Pierre later became Professor of Physics at Sorbonne University. Marie was also interested in chemistry and physics, and was largely the moving power behind the researches of her husband. In collaboration with him, she discovered radium in 1898.

Many years before, Marie had started herself and her husband out on that long, tedious, yet glorious road of accomplishment, at the end of which was to be the discovery of radium. Radium is an almost magic element; it has many constructive uses, including the treatment of disease. They knew that radium existed in a low grade uranium ore called pitchblende. However, to prove to others that it existed and then to be able to isolate it for practical use, was another matter.

For many years, the Curies lived in an attic and worked in a cold, dilapidated, leaky shed which no one else would use. They were without money and their apparatus was all very primitive. They received little or no help from anyone, and were not funded, either by men or science, or by the state. Yet these two "gentle fanatics" worked on alone in a kind of dream-like absorption.

The government was too busy spending money on armaments to buy the Curies the few tons of pitchblende that they needed. But somehow, as in most all cases of this kind, they got their own pitchblende, paying for its transportation themselves out of their insufficient salaries.

With "terrible patience," Marie did the work of four men. She pounded away day after day at her chemical masses, boiling, separating, refining, stirring, and straining. She knew that somewhere in this inert brown substance, radium would someday be found. She went without food and sleep for long periods in her anxiety to learn the secret that she knew must be there.

After their 487th experiment had failed, Pierre threw up his hands in despair and said, "It will never be done. Maybe in a hundred years, but never in our day." Marie confronted him with a resolute face and said, "If it takes a hundred years it will be a pity, but I will not cease to work for it as long as I live."

Such determination and persistence must always be rewarded, and finally success came. The element of radium was isolated and established in the world as one of the most interesting and useful elements. The Curies were now triumphant. With their own hands, brains, and hearts, they had brought about one of the greatest discoveries ever made in the world. Their discovery could have easily made them wealthy for life. But Marie said, "No, radium is one of nature's elements. It is not ours. It belongs to the world."

One of the first decisions the Curies made was that they would not patent their process of extraction, but rather they would give it freely to help science cure disease and assist everyone in the world who needed its help. This decision alone was enough to entitle them to live forever in the hearts of their fellow men. This great quality gave a depth and a strength to their lives which does not attach to the careers of very many people. The Curies were far more than merely great scientists; the devotion of their lives to an ideal matches the religious fervor of some of the greatest spiritualists.

As they worked to isolate the element of radium for our benefit, they also did something much more. They uncovered for our examination far more important human "elements" which were a part of their own lives. Most of the motivations that we use for our own success come from someone else. And here is an inspiring example of devotion to a cause that we can make a part of ourselves.

The Curie's discovery is one of the truly great success stories of the world. Against every kind of obstacle, these humble, self-made people brought an inestimable benefit to all mankind. The discovery itself is worth so very much, but the value of their inspiration and example is worth even more. Here we have evidence that a worthy task often ends with success when it is underwritten and backed up by those human resources found in great people with a Curie-like devotion.

In 1903, the Curies were jointly awarded the Nobel Prize and they continued their work and research. Unfortunately, Pierre was run over by a truck and killed instantly on April

19, 1906. After his death, Marie took over his position at the Sorbonne. In 1911, she was again awarded the Nobel Prize, being the only person who has been so honored twice.

Madame Curie almost went blind, her hands and arms were scarred, pitted, and burned by thirty years of radium emanations. Yet she continued her work almost to the day of her death in 1934. Her death was caused, in part, by the very element which she had worked so hard to release for the use of the world. Madame Curie died, but her discovery did not die; it continues its work of saving the lives of thousands of people every year.

Radium is quite a different kind of element from all others, as the price partially indicates. Radium radiates heat and light and energy. It is translucent. It seems to have been composed from the sunlight. It shines out in the darkness. It penetrates and heals. If you mix a very small part of radium with many parts of an especially- prepared phosphorescent zinc sulphide, a luminescent material is produced which can be applied to the dials of watches and other surfaces to make them highly visible in the dark. Its greatest use, however, remains the destruction of one of man's worst enemies, cancer.

With a little imagination, we might find another use for this wonder element, radium. It might well be a symbol of that "human element" which so often makes human beings "radio- active." Some people have this quality more than others. Like radium, they radiate energy, light, and the power of healing.

There can be developed in people a more or less mysterious power that can keep them going without food, rest, or compensation until the job is done. It can also give them the strength, even while living and working in poverty, to refuse to profit from their labor. Such an attitude toward life, when found in human beings, is like radium among the elements. It also seems to have been composed from the sunlight.

Radium is one of the 117 elements found in nature. Some of the others are hydrogen, oxygen, nitrogen, carbon, iron, etc. Each has its special purpose and use. Each is valuable in some special place. Radium seems to be a little more glamorous than some of the other elements. It kills disease and has life and power.

Still by far, the most valuable elements are those "human elements" found in people. Some of these are kindness, friendliness, integrity, industry, courage, faith, enthusiasm, persistence, and godliness. It is the human elements that not only discover the natural element, but they also give them value and direction. Without our human elements, the elements of nature would have little use.

It is an interesting thought that radium has always existed, and yet the world had gone for thousands of years without benefiting from it, or even knowing of its existence. Only when the human elements of diligence, intelligence, and persistence in someone like Madame Curie go to work do the elements of nature find their usefulness and value.

In this, we also see some comparisons with our own human elements. We have a lot of invaluable resources mixed up in the worthless pitchblende of our lives which we never even learn to understand, much less to isolate and use effectively. We need some human iron in the personality to give it strength, but even iron must be refined by use so as to serve us most effectively. When we are at our best, we refine and develop each one of these human elements in much the same manner as Madame Curie did radium. Only then can we put them to their most constructive use.

The one element that we ought to be particularly careful to get the maximum use from is our "personality radium." We ought to first know the source of our own supply, and then learn how to utilize it to the limit. Every successful personality needs the quality that radiates energy that gives off light and makes us radio-active. Every human being has a radioactive potentiality with a "fall out" that benefits everyone. This quality that we might call "human radium" is also the element that kills personality disease and keeps us in our most vigorous mental and personality health.

One of the most important parts of success is to get our own various personality elements identified and isolated into a form of such purity as to give them maximum power. We ought not to forget that success must come at last to everyone who has those qualities of diligence, imagination, and determination that radiate light and enthusiasm. They are like very valuable drops of sunlight. They make the personality sparkle and shine. But an important thing to remember is that they don't help us much if we don't get them located and then make them negotiable in our own lives.

NAPOLEON THE GREAT

*"I may lose battles,
but no one will ever see
me lose minutes."*

O ne of the strongest men ever to play a part upon the
stage of this world went by the name of Napoleon
the Great. Napoleon possessed many superior qualities. One
was his great ambition. His mind was always full of titanic
schemes. Napoleon was not petty. He made no little plans,
and for many years he held France and much of the world in
the vice of his iron grip. While he was emperor, the rudder of
the ship of state was held by strong hands.

Napoleon the Great also had intense self-confidence.
Answering the question, "What is happiness?" he said, "It is
the highest possible development of myself." He said, "I may
lose battles, but no one will ever see me lose minutes, either
by overconfidence or sloth."

He was a man with a firm grip on the sword hilt,
though he clearly understood the limitations of the sword. He
said, "The sword will always be conquered by the spirit." A
large part of what he achieved was through the power of his
words and the control which he exercised over the emotions of

men.

He lived days of intense glory. He faced death on sixty battle fields. His mind loved to luxuriate in the light of his own supreme ego. He developed such a great spiritual force that it took possession of his soul. Someone has said that the light which radiated from Napoleon was so strong that it could kill. His allusion to his star provided a phrase in which his self-esteem could revel. He said, "I am the god of battles. I have 50,000 men. Add myself and I have 150,000."

It was said by the Duke of Wellington that in his opinion, Napoleon's presence on the field of battle was actually the equivalent of a hundred thousand additional troops. His very name had acquired a mythical power. And his supreme confidence in himself was transferred, as if by magic, to those serving under his command.

Napoleon was supreme because of his supreme efficiency. When he spoke, everyone listened, for he always spoke as an expert. Ambition was the very mainspring of his life. He said, "A man of temperament who aspires and works unceasingly can achieve everything that he can achieve who is vaguely spoken of as a genius." He declared, "Genius is industry."

"Work is my element, it is that for which I have been created," said Napoleon. And work he did, day and night. He once said, "I cannot sleep when I have plans in my head that are not yet on the maps." He would have his secretary come in at any hour to record the master's night thoughts. "If at two in the morning a good idea enters my mind, in a quarter of an hour I have issued my orders and half an hour later my outposts are alerted."

At another time, Napoleon said, "I am always at

work. I think a great deal. If I appear to be ever-ready and equal to every occasion, it is because I have thought over matters long before I undertake to do the slightest thing. I have foreseen every eventuality. There exists no guardian angel who suddenly and mysteriously whispers in my ear what I am to do or say. Everything is turned over in my mind again and again. This is always true, whether I am at the table or at the theatre or in my bed. At night I wake up in order to work. "

What a force was coiled up in the brain of Napoleon. He knew his business. He asked counsel of no one. He did his homework. He never blundered into success. He believed in Napoleon. His favorite rhetoric lay in allusion to "his star, " and he pleased to style himself "The child of destiny. " He put forth all of his strength. He spared nothing–neither ammunition, nor money, nor troops, nor generals, nor himself. He was not blood thirsty, or cruel, but he knew no impediment to his will and woe to the thing or person that stood in his way. His life was highly concentrated, well-focused, and one-directional.

Napoleon was willing to risk everything on his ventures because he knew there was almost no possibility of failure if he kept his objective constantly in view. He was accustomed to overcoming every obstacle. He knew that in view of the thoroughness with which every detail had been planned, there was almost no possibility of failure.

He had a great love for his soldiers, second only to the love of himself and his purpose. He said, "I deem ingratitude to be the greatest weakness any man can have. " Napoleon loved war as a fine art, just as he loved power. His great personal force was accompanied by an immense capacity for sustained concentration. He was called "organized victory. "

Someone once said of him that he was made of granite with a volcano inside. He had an iron purpose and a heart of steel. Emil Ludwig said of him, "We feel in his presence as if we were standing in front of the iron door which guards a glowing human heart, and that we are looking through the keyhole into the fiery furnace of a soul. "

He was one of those hard-driving, one-directional, consolidated persons who concentrated all of the elements of his personal life into one fiery purpose. He focused his life. He achieved centrality in his purpose. Psychologically speaking, he was all in one piece. He illustrates the idea that success is not like a broom with a multitude of straws, but it is concentrated like a bayonet in point and power. His conviction, constancy, and calculation was inspiring.

Napoleon could not be classified as a good man, but he was certainly a strong man. He was a man with an effective personality that always got things done. He was not only a great general, but he was also a powerful human being. All exhibitions of power are fascinating, and perfect integration always results in power.

Napoleon had a remarkable singleness of purpose. It is an attractive spectacle to see even the life of a strong sinner so powerfully organized and so exactly focused that he can hold the minds of millions. In the life of Napoleon is much to be imitated and much to be shunned. The fact that he died an outcast, scorned and hated, was because he also had great weaknesses accompanying his great strengths.

But Napoleon was always a good soldier. No matter what the opposition, he could always be depended upon to work his way to the front. He gave himself over completely to his passion to achieve. He said, "I fan the flames that burn me. "

Napoleon believed that for one to make history he must first know history. So he nourished his mind with the study of great books and great authors. His problem was that he worked for the wrong cause. His purpose was slanted in the wrong direction. He was one of those who had a "damaged soul. " And he was responsible for more deaths, more broken homes, and more suffering than any man of his time.

It has been said that all genius is excess. Napoleon knew no moderation. That was a part of his undoing. Napoleon was the victim of a bad cause, and he was felled by his own hand. We can only wonder what he might have accomplished if this tremendous effort had been used in some worthwhile direction.

There are many great benefits due us from the life of Napoleon. One is that he serves our need for a large scale model of one kind of mistake that we should avoid. Many years ago Colonel Robert G. Ingersoll described the tragedy of Napoleon's life in the most eloquent terms.

He said, "A little while ago I stood by the grave of the old Napoleon—a magnificent tomb of gilt and gold, fit almost for a deity dead. I gazed upon the sarcophagus of rare and nameless marble, where lay at last the ashes of that restless man. I leaned over the balustrade and thought about the career of the greatest soldier of the modern world.

"I saw him walking upon the banks of the Seine contemplating suicide. I saw him at Toulon— I saw him putting down the mob in the streets of Paris—I saw him at the head of the army of Italy—I saw him crossing the bridge of Lodi with the tricolor in his hand—I saw him in Egypt in the shadows of the pyramids—I saw him conquer the Alps and mingle the eagles of

France with the eagles of the crags. I saw him at Marengo–at Ulm and at Austerlitz. I saw him in Russia, where the infantry of the snow and the cavalry of the wild blast scattered his legions like winter's withered leaves. I saw him at Leipsig in defeat and disaster–driven by a million bayonets back upon Paris–clutched like a wild beast–banished to Elba. I saw him escape and retake an empire by the force of his genius. I saw him upon the frightful field of Waterloo, where Chance and Fate combined to wreck the fortunes of their former king. And I saw him at St. Helena, with his hands crossed behind him, gazing out upon the sad and solemn sea.

"I thought of the widows and orphans he had made–of the tears that had been shed for his glory, and of the only woman who ever loved him, pushed from his heart by the cold hand of ambition. And I said to myself I would rather have been a French peasant and worn wooden shoes. I would rather have lived in a hut with a vine growing over the door, and the grapes growing purple in the kisses of the autumn sun. I would rather have been that poor peasant with my loving wife by my side, knitting as the day died out of the sky–with my children upon my knees and their arms about me– I would rather have been that man, and gone down into the tongueless silence of the dreamless dust, than to have been that imperial impersonation of force and murder, known as 'Napoleon the Great.'"

Napoleon was born August 15, 1769. He was a Brigadier General at age 25. At age 35 he was crowned Emperor. Pope Pius the VII came from Rome to the Notre Dame Cathedral in Paris to officiate in the coronation. At the last moment, Napoleon grasped the crown from the Pope and put it upon his own head. During his short lifetime, Napoleon's unbridled imagination wandered across the world and conquered much of it. Napoleon the Great was a great leader of men, but he was also ruthless and immoral. He made his way to emperor over broken oaths and through a sea of blood.

But finally and inevitably came Waterloo and exile. At age 46, he was banished to St. Helena, a small island made up largely of an extinct volcano located in the Atlantic Ocean forty-five hundred miles south of France and twelve hundred miles west of Africa. This little pinpoint in the ocean was referred to as "the Rock. " But even there, the enemies of Napoleon seemed to hold his tremendous initiative and ability in great awe. He was constantly guarded by guns of three thousand British soldiers who were also kept on this small, desolate island at great expense to guard this one single, unarmed human being. Napoleon lived on the Rock under the most unspeakable circumstances for more than two thousand days and nights, or a total of six years. His campaigns in Egypt and Italy had taken only one-half that much time. On St. Helena he lived alone just as he had always been alone. Though constantly in the midst of men, he had no companions.

During his last years, the sense of demoniac loneliness that had accompanied him through life was increased by the consciousness of his failure. He said, "Do not think that I have no terrible moments. I wake up at night and think of what I was and what I have become. Yet no one but myself can be blamed for my fall. I have been my own greatest enemy, the cause of my own disastrous fate. The trappings have now been stripped from me and everyone can judge me in my nakedness. What a pitiful creature I have become. "

Then, with his philosophical mood turned upon himself, he said, "All great men are like meteors who, while they last, light up the sky until they are burned out. " Then he who had almost conquered the world and had been the most prominent being in it said, "This is my burned-out hour. " What a tragic moment when any life finds only ashes in its hands with nothing left to hope for or to believe in or to live by or to look forward to.

However, his great heart of steel was steadfast to the end. Napoleon was wrong in his goals, but his effort was brilliant. He tried magnificently. When contemplating his death as the end was drawing near, he said, "When I am dead it is my wish that my ashes shall be laid to rest on the banks of the Seine in the midst of the French people which I have loved so well. " Then he said to the multitude that had lived on the Rock because of him, "When I am gone, then you can all go home to France, and I shall go to meet with my brave warriors in Elysian fields. We shall talk of our battles to Scipio, to Hannibal, to Caesar and to Frederick. "

In his last hours he looked into the world peopled by the shades of his heroes. His request to be buried in France was not immediately granted. Instead he was buried on the Rock and for the next nineteen years a British sentry was posted constantly at his grave.

Napoleon had won and lost half the world, but in his dying visions he saw the Corsican home of his ancestors. Toward morning, in his last hours of life, he murmured in his delirium two distinguishable words, "France" and "Josephine. " Napoleon had won battle after battle as long as he fought for the glory of France, but when he began fighting for the glory of Napoleon, then Waterloo and exile were just around the corner. He had divorced Josephine out of his ambition to father a line of kings, but he used his last breath to whisper her name–Josephine. Of the sons he desired but did not have, he said, "I wish I could be my own posterity. " Napoleon died at 5:49 p. m. on May 5, 1821, while not yet 52 years of age.

Nineteen years after his death, the dead emperor was brought home to Paris and his statue was replaced on the Vendome Column. When this news was brought to his bedridden mother, she said in a toneless voice, "Once more the Emperor is in Paris. "

HORATIO NELSON

"Success was in his blood."

Ｗe often hear of some unusual yet seemingly helpful customs. For example, if you had visited a home in ancient China and let it be known to your host that you greatly admired some particular article he owned, he may just have wrapped that item up and sent it to you as a present. We might think of this custom as being rather unusual, but isn't that exactly what life also does to us?

There is a fundamental law of attraction that says, "That which we love and admire and desire we get. " That is the way we get friends, character personality qualities, and our material possessions. If we love honesty, we get honesty. Like attracts like. That is one of the most powerful laws governing the development of any effective personality.

There are many ways that this law may be used to help bring about our success. Elbert Hubbard wanted to make his own life as successful as possible. He read that Socrates had said, "Know thyself. " He thought that the best way to learn about himself would be to study "human nature" in other people. The study of human nature is the most fascinating of all knowledge. It gives us power, not only with others, but also with ourselves almost automatically.

Mr. Hubbard picked out 140 of what he considered the world's greatest men, and then, one at a time over a period of fourteen years, he studied each of them carefully. He tried to discover what made them good or bad, successful or unsuccessful, loved or hated.

To make these impressions more definite, he wrote down his ideas in fourteen large volumes called, *Little Journeys into the Lives of Great Men.* We may deepen our impressions and clarify our own ideas by recounting them. He prepared these miniature biographies for his own personal benefit, for naturally as he studied he was attracted by certain qualities and a desire to have them. This law of attraction never fails. Those qualities that we love and desire and work for, life wraps them up and sends them to us as presents.

Inasmuch as this is the law, what would you like? You may have your choice. Two of the cornerstones of success in business, or in life, are courage and industry. Supposing, you would like to strengthen these in yourself. All you would need to do is think about these qualities, desire them, and love them. "Ask and you shall receive." Associate with these qualities as they appear in the lives of great men.

Let me give you a part of Mr. Hubbard's visit with Horatio Nelson. Horatio was a poor, sickly orphan boy who became one of the most important men of his day. How did he do it? Rest assured there was a reason for his greatness. See if you can find it and use it. And remember, what you desire you may have. It will be sent to you free of charge.

Horatio Nelson was born in 1758, one of eleven

children. He was left motherless at the age of nine. His father was too poor to support his large family; and so Horatio, the sickliest of the brood, went to sea as a stowaway at the age of twelve.

It was a rough life for a small boy, but we have a way of rising to meet whatever situations may confront us. Horatio decided he would do his man's job better than anyone else did. Mr. Hubbard said of him, "His quickness in obeying, his alertness and ability to climb, his scorn of danger, going to the yardarm to adjust a tangled rope in a storm, or fastening the pennant to the mast in less time then anyone else on board could perform the task, made him a marked man. He did the difficult thing, the unpleasant thing, with an amount of good cheer that placed him in a class by himself. He had no competition. Success was in his blood. His silent, sober ways, intent only on doing his duty, made his services sought after by every captain who was fitting out a ship for a dangerous undertaking." How wonderful to develop these great qualities, and how much they help us in any undertaking.

Nelson made a trip to the Arctic and came back as second mate at age 19. He was a lieutenant at 20, a lieutenant commander at 21, and a captain at 23 in charge of his own ship. On one occasion, the Prince of Denmark came aboard his ship and asked for the captain. The Prince said, "I was shown a boy in a captain's uniform, the youngest man to look upon I ever saw holding a like position. His face was gaunt and yellow, his chest flat, and his legs absurdly thin. But on talking with him, I saw he was a man who knew what he was doing. When he showed me the ship, he pointed out the cannons saying, 'These are for use if necessity demands.' And there was a gleam in his blue eyes that backed up his words. I knew he meant what he said. "

Before he was twenty- six years old, Nelson had fought pirates, savages, Spaniards, and the French. Physically he was too weak to meet his competitors on that level, so he pitted his brain against their brawn. He studied while his companions gambled and caroused and "saw the town. "

Sir William Hamilton, British Envoy at the Court of Naples, said after meeting Nelson for the first time, "The world will yet ring with the name of Horatio Nelson. " Admiral Hood said of him, "Nelson is the only absolutely invincible fighter in the British Navy. "

From 1793 to 1798, Nelson made history and made it rapidly. He was in constant pursuit of the enemy, giving them no respite from danger, night or day. When a ship mutinied, Horatio was placed in charge of it if he was within call. He once said to a sullen, mutinous crew, "Our enemies are there, and I am depending upon you to follow me over the side and annihilate them. You shall accept no danger that I do not accept, no hardship shall be yours that shall not be mine. I need no promise from you that you will do your duty. I know you will. You believe in me and I in you. We are Englishmen, fighting our country's battles, and so to your work, my men, to your work. "

The mutinous spirit melted away, for the men knew that if Nelson fought with them, it would be for the privilege of getting at the enemy first. No officer ever carried out sterner discipline with his men or with himself, and none was more implicitly obeyed.

Nelson lost an eye in battle in 1795. A few months after, in a fierce engagement, the admiral on the flag ship decided to surrender to the enemy and signaled to Nelson to have his men "stop firing." Nelson's attention was called to the signal and his reply was, "I am short one eye and the other isn't much good, and I accept no signals I cannot see." Then he gave the order to his men, "Lay alongside that ship and sink her."

Nelson was advanced step by step until he became Admiral of the Fleet. At the Battle of Santa Cruz, he led a night attack. Standing in the prow of a small boat, his left arm was shattered at the elbow. He insisted on going forward and continued to command, even though his sword arm was useless.

Finally the loss of blood forced his attendants to take him back to his ship for medical treatment. When he arrived, the surgeons were already busy caring for other wounded. Seeing their commander, the surgeons rushed to his assistance. He ordered them back, declaring he would take his place in line and wait his turn. And this he did.

When it came his turn, the surgeons saw that his arm was shattered and the whole right hand reduced to a pulp, and that amputation was the only thing. There were no anesthetics, and Nelson watched the surgeons sever the worthless arm. As they bandaged the stump, he dictated a report of the battle to his secretary. But after writing for ten minutes, the poor secretary fell in a faint, and Nelson ordered one of the surgeons to complete taking the dictation. The final report contained no mention of the calamity that had befallen the commander. He regarded the loss of an arm as merely an incident in the great cause of winning his country's battles.

In six months he had met and defeated all of the ships of Napoleon that could be located. When he returned to England, an ovation met him such as never before had been given to any seaman. He walked with a limp. No one knew for sure whether it was because they had pinned on him so many medals or, as somebody said, the limp may have been caused by undiscovered lead that had been shot into his body. With one eye and one arm gone, this naturally slender and gaunt figure had a pathetic appearance. But what is visible to the eye is not always the most important part of a great man.

With Napoleon's fleet destroyed, Lord Nelson partially retired from service. But it was not long before Napoleon got together another navy and also recruited the navy of Spain in his cause, so that the combined fleet far outclassed that of England. When they looked for someone who could win against Napoleon, they could think of only one man in England who could, with any assurance of success, fight this great and superior foe on the water. So again Nelson was placed in charge of the British Fleet.

Nelson fought ships as an expert plays chess. He had reduced the game to a science. If the enemy made this move, he made that. He knew how to lure a hostile fleet and have it pursue him to the ground he selected, and then he knew how to cut it in half and whip it piecemeal. His fighting was consummate strategy, combined with a seeming recklessness that gave courage to the troops which made them invincible. What a thrilling thought to contemplate that a man may develop these personality qualities.

The very night Nelson accepted the assignment to fight Napoleon's navies; he started out for the battle. Within four days, he was off the coast of Spain. For the next two-and-a-half years, he was the center and the controlling scene in Trafalgar Bay near the straits of Gibraltar. The Battle of Trafalgar was fought on October 28, 1805.

On the morning of that crucial day, Nelson said, "England expects this day every man to do his duty." He hoisted the signal and gave the order to "close in." And the game of death began.

While the ships were getting into position, he retired to his cabin and wrote out his will, which closed with these words: "May God bless my King and Country and all those I hold dear . . . signed Nelson."

Nelson's own ship led the attack. By noon two enemy ships were on fire and four were making a desperate effort to escape the fate that Nelson had prepared for them. At one o'clock, Nelson's own ship grappled the flag ship of the enemy and chained her fast. The enemy flag ship was shot full of holes and set on fire.

Just at this time a musket ball, fired from the enemy decks, struck Nelson through the shoulder and passed down through the vertebrae. He fell upon the deck, exclaiming to Captain Hardy who was near, "They have done for me now, Hardy. My back is broken."

He was carried below, but the gush of blood into the lungs told the tale. Nelson was dying. The commotion on the deck told him that the enemy flag ship had surrendered. A gleam of joy came into the one blue eye of the dying man; and he said, "I would like to live just one hour more–just to know that my plans were right. We must capture or destroy 20 French ships."

After Nelson had died, Captain Hardy covered his face and the admiral stars on his breast with a handkerchief so that his men would not recognize the dead form of their chief as they hurried by at their work. Nelson was dead, but Trafalgar, one of the pivotal battles of the world, had been won. The courage and skill of Lord Nelson had saved England from the clutches of the "great scourge of Europe," Napoleon.

Nelson knew how to do three things well–how to plan, how to fight, and how to die. He loved and desired and lived great qualities of personality that became his own, according to the universal law of attraction. Their value in his life is evidenced by the fact that as William Pitt said of him, "The name of Nelson will be known as long as governments exist and history is read."

Remember the law of attraction, "That which we love and admire and desire, we get."

JESUS OF NAZARETH

Nothing Can Bring us Peace, but a Triumph of Principles

C hristmas is the time of the year when we commemorate the birth of the greatest life that was ever lived. The most important considerations of our individual existence center in Him who is known to us as Jesus Christ the Son of God. Next to the Father himself, the Son was, and is, the greatest intelligence in the universe. He was commissioned to be the Savior of the world and to redeem all men from death upon condition of repentance. He lived the perfect life and established the pattern for us to follow.

The most important general force in our lives is often the uplifting effect that others may have upon us. Certainly there are very few under takings more profitable than to study the biographies of great men and women. As we become familiar with the best traits in the lives of others, we naturally appropriate their ideas and adapt their virtues for our own use.

This borrowing process achieves its highest significance at this particular season of the year. It is at Christmastime that

135

we most effectively hold up before our minds the great virtues and noble characteristics of the greatest man who ever lived.

We think of greatness partly in terms of what it has already accomplished and partly in terms of what it promises for the future. We might most profitably begin our Christmas consideration of the life of the Master by a mental excursion back into His pre-existence.

Jesus was the first begotten Son of God in the spirit. Paul referred to Him as the "first born among many brethren. " (Romans 8:28) And He was chosen to be the Savior of the world and the Redeemer of an unborn race of mortals because He was the best qualified for that all-important responsibility. It was decided in the Council of Heaven that this preeminent Son of God should come into the world, and take upon Himself our sins, and do the other necessary things for us that we could not do for ourselves.

Over seven centuries before Christ, the Prophet Isaiah foretold His birth. As he looked into the future he said, "For unto us a child is born, unto us a Son is given: and the government shall be upon his shoulder: and his name shall be called Wonderful, Counsellor, The Mighty God, The Everlasting Father, and The Prince of Peace. Of the increase of his government and peace there shall be no end. . . (Isaiah 9:6, 7)

We are all aware of the significance that a name or a title may have in describing an important office. Isaiah used the wonderful titles of Savior and Redeemer. He referred to Him as the "Mighty God, the Everlasting Father. " It was by His intelligence and power that worlds were organized and their laws and order established. This magnificent personage is known in the Old Testament as Jehovah, the God of Abraham,

136

Isaac and Jacob. Isaiah also called him "Wonderful," and "Counsellor." How appropriate it would be to remove the comma and call Him a Wonderful Counsellor.

Jesus taught that He came so that we might have life and have it more abundantly. And in His attempt to give us a more abundant life, He was given over fifty other important titles such as: the Great Physician, the Great Teacher, the Light of the World, the Door of the Sheepfold, the Good Husbandman, and many others.

Finally He was placed on trial, not only for His life, but also for His way of life. Just think how the lives of everyone would be transformed if we actually followed His pattern. Suppose that we followed the counsel that He gave from the top of Mount Sinai, when out of the fire and smoke, accompanied by the lightnings and thunders of that holy mountain, Jehovah gave those ten great commandments beginning with that one which said, "Thou shalt have no other gods before me." Think what quality would be given to our lives if we actually lived the Sermon on the Mount or obeyed the many other commandments He has given us.

Just suppose that the Golden Rule and God's marriage covenant were fully applied to our individual lives. Then suppose that we made ourselves familiar with every other truth that He has given and anxiously put into actual operation His high standards of honor, integrity and righteousness.

There is no one to whom we owe a greater debt than to Him whose birth we commemorate at the Christmas season. Not only were we created in God's image, but each of us has been endowed with a set of His gifts and potentialities. One of His most stimulating titles, and one that is of particular interest to our present world, is the one where Isaiah called him "The Prince of Peace." And Isaiah said of the increase of His government and peace, there shall be no end. What a thrilling hope for a war-weary, sin-laden world.

Seven hundred years after Isaiah had spoken these words, a great concourse of angels came to the earth to announce Christ's birth and re-proclaim His title. Luke described their appearance to the shepherds tending their flocks upon the Judean hills as follows:

> And there were in the same country shepherds abiding in the field, keeping watch over their flock by night.
>
> And, lo, the angel of the Lord came upon them, and the glory of the Lord shone round about them: and they were sore afraid.
>
> And the angel said unto them, Fear not: for, behold, I bring you good tidings of great joy, which shall be to all people.
>
> For unto you is born this day in the city of David, a Savior, which is Christ the Lord.
>
> And this shall be a sign unto you; ye shall find the babe wrapped in swaddling clothes, lying in a manger.
>
> And suddenly there was with the angel a multitude of the heavenly host praising God, and
>
> saying, 'Glory to God in the highest, and on earth peace, good will toward men.' (Luke 2:8-14)

Since that day, over twenty wide centuries have come and gone, and yet the angelic promise of peace on earth, good will toward men has never yet been realized. In fact, it has seemed that the very opposite has been true. Rather than peace, these twenty centuries have been filled with apostasy, frustrations, evil, disbelief and war. And certainly no age can compare in strife and unrest with the present day. There exist some powerful men in the world who are devoting themselves to keeping their people in a state of constant turmoil and unrest. Satan himself is our most persistent troublemaker, and he is followed by all of those who work for wickedness, and unrighteous dominion with no other primary purpose than that of causing contention, unpleasantness, and misery.

While every honest person condemns trickery and duplicity, there are many people who in their daily lives are more inclined to follow the trouble- makers than to follow the Prince of Peace. There are few of us who excel as peacemakers and truly follow the one ordained of God to be the Prince of Peace. While under Satan, some evil people operate their trouble making upon a broad international scale. Some of us may also be guilty of this same sin of dissension in our more limited spheres. Sin always destroys peace; and frequently through our unrighteousness, we sow the seeds of disagreement and unhappiness. The individual and the home are the most common scenes of strife and bitterness among people. There can never be peace and good will in lives or in homes where sin flourishes. For a very good reason, no sin is ever tolerated in the presence of God. Neither should it be tolerated in our presence and certainly not in our conduct.

A young mother recently had a nervous breakdown because of the deceit, irresponsibility, and unrighteousness in her husband. He seemed to match, on a personal basis, the duplicity and trouble making abilities of some of our ungodly dictators. It is no small thing to make a hell for our wives and children. Kindness and consideration for others are among the greatest Christian virtues. And these were among the virtues always practiced by the Prince of Peace, even while He was upon the cross.

Recently I reread *The Life of Mohandas K. Gandhi*, by Louis Fischer. Although Gandhi was not a Christian, he was often described as one of the most Christ-like of men. His chief characteristic was peace. Almost single handedly, he won the independence of India, entirely by non-violent means. He would tolerate no falsehood or threat of force in himself or in any of his followers. He would far rather suffer wrong than do wrong. His motive was happiness for others, even though they made him suffer pain or imprisonment. Then on that fateful evening of January 30, 1948, as he was walking to the prayer ground for his evening devotion, he was shot by a crazed fanatic. Gandhi lived just long enough to forgive his assassin and pronounce a blessing upon him.

Nineteen hundred years earlier, from the top of Mount Calvary, Jesus has said of His own assassins, "Father, forgive them; for they know not what they do. " Jesus earned the right to be called the Prince of Peace because He taught and lived the gospel of peace. By actually living the principles of peace is the only way that peace can be brought to the individual heart or to the world in general.

Gandhi's last act before dying was to raise his hands and bless his assassin. But during the entire life of Jesus, His mission was to bless people, and one of His main beatitudes was, "Blessed are the peacemakers for they shall be called the children of God. " (Matthew 5:9) What a marvelous title to which we ourselves may aspire, and what a thrilling example for us to follow.

Because we do not all understand the real significance of Christmas, it comes to mean different things to different people. We have the child's Christmas. Its symbol is the toy, and its chief characteristic is excitement. Then there is the world's Christmas. Its symbol is the Christmas tree, and its chief characteristic is festivity. There is the drunkard's Christmas. Its symbol is the bottle, and its chief characteristic is sin. Then there is the Christian's Christmas. Its symbol is the star, and the chief characteristics are worship, righteousness, peace, and good will.

At this Christmas time, as at each and every Christmas, all of the people of the earth have been searching for peace. Peace can never be attained apart from righteousness. The best way to get peace is by a personal obedience to the Prince of Peace. The crowning perfection of any good Christian is a clear conscience. With a good program of understanding and a righteous personal devotion, there arises in the soul a serenity and peace far surpassing the most satisfying bodily pleasures. Peace and good will are among the most pleasant of earthly delights. Fortunately, the poor can obtain peace as easily as the rich, the social outcasts get it as freely as the leader of society, and the humblest citizen can have a peace equal to those who wield the greatest political power.

Jesus has offered us a peace that surpasseth understanding. He said, "Peace I leave with you, my peace I give unto you: not as the world giveth, give I unto you. Let not your heart be troubled, neither let it be afraid." This peace can only come through our fairness, righteousness, and truth. Emerson said, "Nothing can bring us peace, but a triumph of principles." They constitute the program of the Prince of Peace who is also the prince of possibilities, the prince of progress, and the prince of eternal glory.

I would like to close with the salutation of the early Christians, "May the God of peace be with you. " (Romans 15:33) "Peace be unto your house and peace be unto your soul. " (I Samuel 25:6)

THE PROPHET JOB

Suffering has a Purpose

L ife is that primal element out of which all experiences are formed. Within the human body is housed a miraculous brain, a potentially- magnificent personality, a godly spirit, and the greatest of all future possibilities. A fascinating journey of thought can be experienced as we turn the spotlight of our attention upon the many facets of our God- given human nature and study the interesting interplay of human experience as it reacts upon itself.

One of the most interesting classifications of human beings is that small group of men called the prophets. They are selected by God to assist Him in carrying forward the enterprise of human salvation, yet they are uniquely diverse in their own right. Each has some admirable capabilities and is assigned to serve as God's watchmen, messengers, motivators, teachers, and judges. They also serve as patterns to mankind since we often require a better blueprint than ourselves to follow.

The Holy Scriptures are treasured because of the great religious doctrines and the guidance offered for human behavior. The value of the scriptures has been greatly increased by the fascinating biographies they contain. The scriptures are a kind of God's "Who's Who," and a divine catalog of those men and women whom God entrusted. One of these great men is the Prophet Job.

It has been said that the Old Testament Book of Job furnishes us with the finest expression of the poetic genius of the Hebrews. It has also been accorded a leading place among the greatest masterpieces of world literature. Job himself was an Edomite of outstanding piety, and the theme of his book centers on that eternal question concerning the purpose of human suffering, either merited or not merited. Left to themselves, most men are by nature morally frail, yet one of the purposes of our lives is to be tested, proven, tried, and strengthened.

After all of these centuries since the book was written, we still speak of "the patience of Job," and we are made stronger by that fortitude with which he met the severe suffering that he did not understand. While Christ himself is our greatest example of innocent suffering, yet in his day, Job certainly warranted extreme praise for his almost inhuman endurance.

Patience is one of the traits in shortest supply in our day. We seek instant gratification at every turn. Technology has allowed us to accomplish more; yet we are never satisfied. It is the natural disposition of most people to rebel when events are not to their liking. Instead of a manifestation of love and forbearance, our feelings frequently turn to hate, bitterness, disobedience, and evil.

By this process of mishandling our suffering, many of our greatest blessings are frequently lost. In describing one of the exemplary traits of Jesus scripture says, "Though he were a

Son, yet learned he obedience by the things which he suffered; And being made perfect, he became the author of eternal salvation unto all them that obey him. " (Hebrews 5:8, 9)

If Christ himself was made perfect through suffering, then we should probably know a little more about how to handle this power. There is another very important question asked in the Book of Job which says,

Can a man be profitable unto God, as he that is wise may be profitable unto himself? "Is it any pleasure to the Almighty, that thou art righteous? Or is it gain to him, that thou makest thy ways perfect? (Job 22:2, 3)

If a man does the right things, he can be very profitable unto himself, and he can be very profitable to God.

God's love is centered in us, and He is made happy and prosperous when we are successful. We might try to imagine the joy and profit that Job brought to God. Even among the luminaries that light up the pages of the Holy Scriptures, Job stands out like a great beacon, and he passed all of his tests with supreme devotion.

We are introduced to Job in the first chapter when the record says:

There was a man in the land of Uz, whose name was Job; and that man was perfect and upright, and one that feared God, and eschewed evil.

And there were born unto him seven sons and three daughters.

His substance also was seven thousand sheep, and three thousand camels, and five hundred yoke of oxen, and five hundred she asses, and a very great household; so that this man was the greatest of all the men of the east. (Job 1:1-3)

That sounds pretty good for a start. Job got some recommendation from the fact that he had done well financially and had been successful with his family. The scripture also gave him a top rating in his human relations when it says that ". . . he was the greatest of all the men of the east."

However, Job's greatest credit comes from the fact that he stood well with God. Again the record says:

Now there was a day when the sons of God came to present themselves before the Lord, and Satan came also among them.

And the Lord said unto Satan, Whence contest thou? Then Satan answered the Lord, and said, from going to and fro in the earth, and from walking up and down in it.

And the Lord said unto Satan, Hast thou considered my servant Job, that there is none like him in the earth, a perfect and upright man, one that feareth God, and escheweth evil?

Then Satan answered the Lord, and said, Doth Job fear God for naught?

Hast not thou made an hedge about him, and about his house, and about all that he hath on every side? Thou hast blessed the work of his hands, and his substance is increased in the land.
(Job 1:6-10)

This "hedging about" process based on our obedience seems to be one of the characteristics of God's relationship with us. If we keep His laws of health, we will have strong bodies and clear minds. If we pay our tithing, do our planning, and practice our industry, the Lord will bless us with material abundance. If we keep ourselves mentally, physically, and religiously strong, a great multitude of benefits will be showered upon us. In other words, if we follow His instructions, He usually hedges all of us about on every side. However, Satan argued that it was easy for one to be faithful when everything is going well. But, said he, ". . . put forth thine hand now, and touch all that he hath and he will curse thee to thy face. " (Job 1:11)

This involves our program of testing. And this is frequently the place where so many of us fall down. However, in every field, it seems that challenges and problems are necessary to bring out the sincerity of our character.

Satan was inferring that Job's piety depended upon his prosperity. Satan said, Job doesn't serve God for nothing, and the intimation was that Job's religion was mere selfishness. Many people actually do behave that way. To them, a good religious attitude is merely a profitable business asset. And Satan was suggesting that if God were to withhold His blessings, He would see such a different kind of attitude manifest itself in Job that he would curse God to His face.

Actually, we see this doctrine of weakness manifesting itself every day. The wealthy, powerful nations of our own time, including our own, are trying to buy friendship and cooperation with money. We hand out many benefits in order to get other nations on our side. Many individuals, old and young, must be bribed or they will rebel and join ranks with those who will make their loyalty more profitable.

In Job's case, Satan was accusing God of having a kind of Marshall give- away plan for keeping on the good side of Job. In any event, Satan obtained permission to put Job's loyalty to the test. "And the Lord said unto Satan, Behold, all that he hath is in thy power; only upon himself put not forth thine hand. " (Job 1:12)

Then from the height of his prosperity and happiness, Job was suddenly plunged into the depths of misery and gloom. He lost all of his property, and his children were cut from life by violent deaths. And while Job was profoundly grieved, yet he never wavered, but clung reverently to the will of God.

Then Satan concluded that the test was not severe enough, and he received permission to afflict Job's person to the limit. Job was smitten with a loathsome disease calculated to make him an outcast and an object of abhorrence to other people. But still Job was obedient to God, and his faith remained unbroken.

Within himself, Job reasoned as follows: Shall we receive only good at the hand of God? Apparently, Job felt that he should be willing to bear his share of the problems and suffering as well as to enjoy the blessings.

God must have been very proud of Job when it was proven that he could stand up under the worst hardships, under the most trying adversity that even Satan could devise. Job was content. He said, Naked came I into the world and naked shall I return thither. "The Lord giveth and the Lord taketh away; blessed be the name of the Lord. " (Job 1:21)

Some of Job's friends argued with him, and even his wife got discouraged and seemed about ready to give up. She suggested the formula frequently followed by many people in trouble when she said to her husband, ". . . curse God, and die. " (Job 2:9)

Job didn't understand God, but he was not a quitter.

If God had decreed that he should suffer, that was God's business and He probably had some good reasons for doing as He did. And Job himself was solid and steadfast. He said, "Though he slay me, yet will I trust in him: but I will maintain mine own ways before him. " (Job 13:15) And no matter what the circumstances, Job would continue to do his best.

Frequently problems and suffering serve the best purposes in our lives. In every way, Job trusted God, and naturally God trusted Job. He had already said that Job was an upright man, and Job proved that God did not have him overrated. In the midst of these serious troubles, Job made a magnificent speech to himself. He said,

All the while my breath is in me, and the spirit of God is in my nostrils;

My lips shall not speak wickedness, nor my tongue utter deceit.

. . . till I die I will not remove mine integrity from me.

My righteousness I hold fast, and will not let it go: my heart shall not reproach me so long as I live. (Job 27:3-6)

And we might shout, "Hurrah for Job! " Then we might try to imagine what a tremendous boost our world would get if we had about 6 billion people just like him. Any such man would be very profitable to himself. He would be profitable to God, and he would be profitable to his fellowmen.

Job held on to his integrity, but he also held on to his consistency. Speaking of God, he said, "He also shall be my salvation: for an hypocrite shall not come before him. "

(Job 13:16) Job not only had strong personal convictions within himself, but he was also anxious to get some of these convictions into other people for their own benefit. Answering the question, "If a man die, shall he live again?" Job said:

> Oh that my words were now written! Oh that they were printed in a book!
>
> That they were graven with an iron pen and lead in the rock for ever!
>
> For I know that my redeemer liveth, and that he shall stand at the latter day upon the earth:
>
> And though after my skin worms destroy this body, yet in my flesh shall I see God:
>
> Whom I shall see for myself, and mine eyes shall behold, and not another; though my reins be consumed within me. (Job 19:23-27)

Job knew a great deal about God's plan for our eternal salvation. He also knew a great deal about God and about himself. He said, ". . . there is a spirit in man: and the inspiration of the Almighty giveth them understanding." He knew that we are all likely to err unless we follow instructions. He said, "Great men are not always wise: neither do the aged understand judgment." (Job 32:8, 9) Job was a great man, and he knew what some of us may *not* know—that all of our human wisdom is weak when compared to the wisdom of God.

We would do well to follow the example of Job in his faith. After Job had passed all of his tests, he was given twice as much as he had previously owned before. The record says, "So the Lord blessed the latter end of Job more than his beginning: . . . " (Job 42:12) May God help us to be faithful so that we may merit the appropriate reward!

SOCRATES

"Know thyself."

B y reading books we can enjoy a familiarity with the greatest people of all ages; a familiarity which might have been impossible even to their next-door neighbors of the time period. We often tend to appropriate for ourselves the quotations that were spoken and the concepts that were taught by people, who long ago, were held in high esteem by society and who are now worthy of our emulation. This process seasons our minds and sharpens our opinions, allowing us to access a library of thought that never closes. Interestingly enough, we often visit this timeless treasure without the slightest recognition that the ideas we are recalling actually belong to someone else.

One such important benefactor of wisdom was the ancient Greek philosopher, Socrates. He lived for seventy-one years in Athens, beginning in the year 470 B. C. , and is credited with the introduction of the dialectic method of inquiry known as the "Socratic Method. " At the time, he largely applied this questioning to the examination of key moral concepts such as what is good and what is just. Socrates believed that by first asking questions to determine underlying beliefs, one could then get at the truth more quickly. This method was later adapted to science and was termed the "Scientific Method," which is a process of formulating a question or hypothesis in order to test possible outcomes.

Socrates was the son of Sophroniscus, who was a stonemason. Following the trade of his father, Socrates dabbled in work, but found that his pursuit of virtue and strict adherence to truth pulled at him with a divine like power. He wanted nothing more than to educate the citizens of Athens in the principles of goodness, beauty, and virtue. Appropriately enough, he was the first man to whom the term "philosopher" was applied, which means "a lover of wisdom."

To love wisdom is to have the ability to judge soundly and deal effectively with facts, especially as they relate to society as a whole. Because Socrates found joy in reasoning, he devoted his life to philosophy. It gave him an overwhelming sense of satisfaction to feel a maturity developing within himself, and he was gratified as he saw virtues increasing in others. One of the secrets of his successful life was that he treasured knowledge, understanding, fairness, and righteousness. He never actually claimed to be wise. Instead, he claimed to understand the path that a lover of wisdom must take in pursuing it.

Socrates spoke of having received promptings from an inner voice acting as a divine mentor directing him to do right and that seemed to be training his conscience. He said that from the time of his childhood, this unseen mentor had always forbidden him to do any kind of evil. When a friend insisted he remain silent to avoid a disagreement, Socrates said, "I cannot hold my tongue, as it would be a disobedience to a divine command. " A favorite doctrine of Socrates was that learning is mostly remembering. He believed that we all lived in a previous existence and that the intelligence attained there can have influence over us now.

Socrates believed that all labor which produced courage in the mind and strength in the soul was good. He felt a sense of divine purpose to help people grow in godliness and often spoke about the immortality of the soul. What a thrilling event it would have been if he could have met with Jesus of Nazareth for a deep philosophical discussion filled with probing questions to life's meaning.

Socrates preceded Jesus in mortality by 470 years, but in many ways closely resembled the Savior. This great philosopher's influence and power did not come from the eloquence of his words so much as from the influence of his extraordinary character. Even a nod from one who is highly esteemed can have more impact than a thousand arguments of studied phrases from a person lacking in strength of soul.

To Socrates, all wickedness was a result of either ignorance or sloth. Certainly, he would admonish the people of our day to learn more and to do more and to value principle over greed. He taught that the first duty of every man was to obey the law and submit to punishment when he was judged to be in error. Our current system of justice, with all of its many loopholes that allow the guilty to escape punishment, would be an abomination to Socrates.

Although most of his life was spent in teaching and reasoning, he never allowed his discussions to become heated or bitter. He always kept perfect control of himself, no matter how badly the argument went against him. Hatred had no place in his life. Common to the period in Greece, was the idea that "might makes right, " and this was one philosophy that he worked tirelessly to undermine because of its opposition to truth.

When the war broke out between Athens and Sparta, Socrates enlisted and quickly set himself apart as a brave warrior, excelling his fellow soldiers in the ease with which he endured hardships. He walked over the winter ice with bare feet and was known to have pulled his belt one hole tighter in lieu of breakfast. These actions were to teach the complaining soldiers that battles could be won with discipline and endurance. These same principles, if applied to the battles in a person's day to day life will yield victory. Socrates tried to keep people working and learning and ever vigilant about their current circumstances. He understood the truth that most men fall asleep at their posts when there is no enemy in the field. Without the constant exercise of the mind through the pursuit of truth, the things that can destroy us are given the advantage.

Socrates did not seek for financial gain from his teachings. He shared his thoughts and his knowledge because he loved wisdom and desired to bring out the best in others as well as in himself. He said, "One man finds pleasure in developing his horses. But pleasure for me lies in seeing myself grow day by day. " Socrates believed that in order to gain wisdom a person must first seek to understand one's own heart. His now infamous motto, "Know thyself, " has come to us across a vast expanse of time and yet endures as one of the most successful techniques for human development. Socrates learned to know himself by observing his reactions when he was thwarted, crossed, contradicted, or deprived of comforts and pleasures. He would try mentally to stand away from himself and watch his own mind work. Should it become confused and angered, he would determine the cause and the insufficiency within that allowed it. He also carefully observed other people and their reactions to particular social stimuli. The mixed motives that we rarely detect in our own acts are often easily recognized in the behavior of others.

These observations, along with all other of his life experiences, whether positive or negative, were considered of value to Socrates because they served to increase his wisdom. The difficult challenges in life or the extreme trials of one's character were not counted as unpleasant, but rather as a privilege. He believed that people who escaped the unfavorable experiences of life were actually cheated out of much that was worthwhile for their learning.

Socrates felt that a philosopher should never speak unless his words were steeped in meaning. Character, he believed, was largely a matter of growth. As a lover of wisdom, he perceived his mission in life was to assist others to think and reason logically for themselves in order to avoid ever being at the mercy of the opinions of others. People traveled long distances to hear him speak. He wanted to bring his listeners out of their ill tempers, their bad habits, and their improper attitudes, into a world of understanding and reason.

In his day, groups of men would meet to discuss problems over dinner. Seeking to teach a principle of truth, Socrates proposed the idea that what we give to the body as food is eventually lost, but what we give to the soul as we discuss and learn and absorb wisdom is kept forever. The importance of sharing wisdom was illustrated by his observation of the seating arrangement of the men who attended these mastermind groups. The men usually sat on the floor in a circle and often leaned against each other for support. Socrates expounded on this example by showing that just as water is made to run from a fuller to an emptier cask by means of a siphon, so wisdom flows from greater to the less among men.

Despite claiming unceasing loyalty to his city, Socrates' pursuit of virtue and his strict adherence to truth clashed with Athenian politics and society. Rather than accepting the development of immorality within his region, Socrates worked to undermine the forces that were attempting to redefine right and wrong. He was referred to as a "gadfly" of the state in so far as he irritated the establishment with considerations of justice and the pursuit of goodness. His attempts to improve the Athenian's allegiance to justice may have been the reason he was condemned to die for his opposition to accept and teach that which was contrary to his beliefs. Socrates was sentenced to death by drinking a mixture made from the poisonous hemlock plant.

We have every reason to believe that this great and admirable man was completely honest when he said, "I care not a straw for death; my only fear is of doing some unrighteous or unholy thing. " Indeed, Socrates proved the mighty strength of his convictions when he was presented with an opportunity to escape. It is recorded that his followers offered to bribe the prison guards, thus providing a way for Socrates to flee his captors. According to Plato, the protégé of Socrates, the idea of escaping was not an option his wise teacher would entertain. Plato revealed that Socrates believed running away from his sentence would indicate a fear of death, which no true philosopher has! Even more astounding, especially in comparison to the attitudes of our current society, Socrates was attributed with saying that he had agreed to live under the city's laws (Athens) and was found guilty by them and would accept his punishment and his fate.

Socrates knew himself. He knew the principles on which he based his every word, his every action, his every promise. He lived what he taught and he loved truth more than he loved his own life. The Socratic Method would dictate that as we seek to understand what can make us rich in life, we might ask the question, "What makes a good man or a good woman?" If Socrates was here to answer us, he would reply, as he did to the Athenians, "A good man ought not to calculate his chances of living or dying. He ought only to consider whether he is doing right or wrong. "

ANTONIO STRADAVARI

A Philosophy of Excellence

One of the most important parts of our success frequently comes through the study of biography. We seem to learn faster from people than from things or abstract ideas. In people, we have an important visual aid, an actual working model where we can see success and failure ready-made. Fortunately for us, everyone has something to teach us. Jesus used the lives of people, both good and bad, to illustrate some of the greatest lessons of life. With substantial profit to ourselves, we can build on this example.

The man whose name provides the title for this chapter was the master violin maker of the world. The traits that will forever identify the name of Stradivari, and make it a household word, were his love of his job and his painstaking effort to give superiority to every work that his hands touched. If practiced, that will also bring greatness, happiness, and success to our lives.

Antonio was born in Cremona, Italy in 1644. He loved music, but he could neither sing nor play a musical instrument.

As a young boy someone gave him a present of a jackknife; and because he wanted something to do, he whittled. His whittling was directed to producing little wooden violins.

There have been a lot of whittlers in the world, and some may have even whittled violins. However, Antonio was different from the others because he whittled perfect violins. To him whittling had a purpose far more important than a mere pastime, and every violin that his jackknife touched had to be completely finished before he laid it down.

It just happened that Cremona was also the home of another famous violin maker, Nicholas Amati. One day, one of Antonio's toy violins fell into Amati's hands. Nicholas knew that some extraordinary person had made it, for the man who loves his job always leaves distinguishing marks on whatever he does. As soon as Amati could find Antonio, Antonio began carving violins for this great master.

From the very beginning this young boy was destined to be famous, for while Antonio was making violins, the violins were making Antonio. What one does, and the way one does it, builds character and forms a priceless philosophy of life that can distinguish the person forever. Quality work is important for many reasons. One is that it soon gets into the worker's muscles and into attitudes, and determines the kind of man he himself will be.

That was also the philosophy of Antonio. Even though he was making violins for someone else, yet he made them with his whole heart. He utilized to the fullest his God-given urge to excel. Antonio felt that he must make better violins than anyone else, even including Amati himself. And that is exactly what he did! It has been said that in over 300 years not one of Stradivari's violins has ever been known to come to pieces or break because of poor workmanship.

When Stradivari began working for himself he needed no patent for his violins, for no other violin maker paid as great a price for excellence as did Antonio. There was no point in writing his name on his work for it was already stamped in the superiority of every part of every instrument. And every Stradivarius now in existence is worth many times its weight in gold. Whatever our own work may be, we might well memorize Antonio's philosophy of life. He said:

When any master holds
Twixt hand and chin a violin of mine.
He will be glad that Stradivari lived,
Made violins, and made them of the best.

The masters only know whose work is good;
They will choose mine,
And while God gives them skill,
I give them instruments to play upon,
God choosing me to help Him,
For God could not make Antonio Stradivari's violins
Without Antonio.

A philosophy of excellence underlines and determines one of the most important principles of any success. Nicholas Latena has said, "One may possibly be better than his principles." Life will grant us any desire that is built upon a sufficient love of what we are doing and supported by a firm determination to do it well. This philosophy not only produces excellence in every accomplishment, but it also does away with worker fatigue and gives vigor and grace to life itself.

By way of contrast, we might look at the other side of the picture and take the measure of the man who doesn't love his job and consequently does it poorly. It has been said that some men looking for work quit looking the minute they find it. Instead of loving what they are doing, many people hate their jobs.

Jesus pointed to love as the greatest of all of God's commandments, and hate as one of the worst of the sins. When this ugly trait once gets a foothold in our lives, it is carried over into everything we do. Sometimes we live with it for a lifetime without being aware of the terrible things it does to us.

When one's love is not properly nourished, adjusted, and focused, it causes him to go stale on the job. Then he becomes like a child who can only maintain his interest in new toys for a short time, and then he must constantly change playthings if he is to keep himself amused. Antonio worked only with wood and strings and glue, and yet he was never bored while making his violins. His job never lost its freshness, or its challenge.

It has been said that the soul of the lover lives in the body of the object loved. When someone fails to develop a great love centered in something outside himself, then offense and hate grow quickly and tend to turn the hater sour and unsuccessful.

I know a fine young man who worked for an excellent company. He was very enthusiastic and successful for a few years. But his love became too much focused on himself. At first this trait went unrecognized. Then a combination of circumstances, including a little over-confidence, a little unscheduled relaxation of his effort, and a little failure in his

162

interest brought about a weakening in his success.

Soon he began subconsciously to blame others for his decline. He made himself feel that his company and his friends delighted in opposing him. He hopelessly exaggerated in his own mind every unfavorable situation. He took every occasion to dislike the company officers and seemed to get a kind of sadistic pleasure out of his own hate. All of the time he really was the one being most seriously injured. Curses always recoil upon the head of him who sets them in motion.

Some time ago a friend of mine was stung by a bee, and the bee left his stinger in my friend's arm. The sting hurt my friend, but it killed the bee. When we allow any amount of the poison of hate to be generated by us, it soon fills up our system until we can't take it any longer.

We can solve almost every one of our problems by learning to love–to love our jobs, to love the company we work for, to love the people we work with, to love life, to love excellence, to love God. Anyone who works with other people will encounter problems and differences of opinion. But all of the problems can be solved.

We need to recognize that there are no perfect people in the world. Ever since time began, the work of the world has been done by imperfect men in an imperfect way, and will continue to be so done until time ends. If someone makes a mistake, it can be corrected if love is maintained at proper strength.

If we get angry and allow our hate glands to start pumping poison, then we are lost. We increase this poisonous output by thinking about it, agitating its causes, giving voice to our unfavorable opinions about it, and trying to justify it. By these processes we can soon completely destroy our confidence in the best people, or in the best company, or in the government, or in our church, or even in God himself.

How can anyone do good work for a company that he hates, or for leaders in whom he has lost confidence, or for associates for whom he has no regard, or for a God whom he believes to be unfair? One of the best ways he can learn to love his work is to follow the formula of Stradivari, and that is to do the very best that he can.

It was Stradivari's business to build better violins. It is God's business to build better men and women with great character qualities, more determined faith, and more unwavering righteousness. He has invited us to have a part in the work in which He himself spends His entire time. What a tremendous advantage it would give us if we could develop a little better philosophy of life!

In his inaugural address President John F. Kennedy said, "Never ask what your country can do for you, but rather what you can do for your country. " A person who loves his country best, serves it most. A person who loves God, puts his own life in harmony with Him, and serves his fellow men as though his life depends upon it, as indeed it does.

Antonio learned to love his job by doing superior work, and that is the best way for anyone to bring about his own success. Instead of saying so many prayers asking God to do things for us, we ought to say more of our prayers requesting the very things that characterized the greatness of Antonio Stradivari. And then we should work hard to achieve those same characteristics that we prayed so earnestly to receive. We should turn out no shoddy work.

Stradivari's friend, Naldo, once tried to induce Antonio to make more money by turning out a greater number of violins. He argued that Antonio's painstaking efforts were undesirable. Naldo said, "Why work with such a painful nicety?" Stradivari replied:

> My work is mine;
> If my hand slackened, I should rob God.
> I am one best
> Here in Cremona, using sunlight well
> To fashion finest maple till it serve
> More cunningly than throats for harmony,
> 'Tis rare delight; I would not change my skill
> To be an Emperor with bungling hands,
> And lose my work which comes as natural
> As self at waking.

Stradivari said that his violins were made for eternity, and that is exactly the period for which our lives are being fashioned. It would serve us well to accept nothing less than our very best from ourselves. Our lives can become rich in every aspect when excellence is our goal.

BOOKER T. WASHINGTON

*"I expect to have
a successful, pleasant day."*

The usual plot of an interesting movie almost always begins with the hero getting into an impossible situation, and then the rest of the show is watching him try to get out of the "hole" by working up to a happy ending. This is also the pattern of the plot of most successful lives. Creation seems to have a special reason in determining the size of the obstacles we can overcome.

Few men known to history have started lower or climbed higher than did Booker T. Washington. He was born a slave on a plantation in Franklin County, Virginia, in 1858. He knew very little about his mother and nothing at all about his father, except a report that he was a white man who lived on a nearby plantation. His first few years were spent on the dirt floor of a slave cabin. He was born and reared in the lower depths of slavery, ignorance, and poverty. In his childhood he suffered from want of a place to sleep, for lack of food, clothing, and shelter. He said, "I had not had the privilege of sitting down to a table to eat until I was quite well grown.

Luxuries were something meant for white people, not for my race. "

On Sundays he would sometimes be given two spoonfuls of molasses as a special reward. He said, "I would tip the plate in one direction and then another so as to make the molasses spread all over it in the full belief that there would be more molasses and that it would last longer if spread out in this way. So strong were my childish impressions of those Sunday morning 'feasts,' that it would be pretty hard for anyone to convince me even now that there is not more molasses on the plate when it is spread all over the plate than when it just occupies one little corner. These two spoonfuls of molasses were more enjoyable to me then, than any 14-course dinner could have been to one under opposite circumstances. "

He had no schooling whatever while he was a slave and for some time thereafter. He was required to carry the books of his white mistress to the schoolhouse door, but was forbidden to enter the schoolhouse. He said, "I had a feeling that to get into a schoolhouse and study would be about the same as getting into Paradise. Even in those early years I had an intense longing to read, and there was never a time in my life, no matter how dark and discouraging the days might be, when one resolve did not continually actuate my determination, and that was to secure an education at any cost. "

One day a young man who could read moved into the little community where young Booker lived, and it was arranged that Booker should work for him in exchange for being taught how to read. But one day while at work in a coal mine, he happened to overhear two miners talking about a school for "colored people" in Hampton, Virginia. Booker said, "In the darkness of the mine I noiselessly crept close as

I could to the two men who were talking. I heard one tell the other that not only was the school established for Negroes, but that opportunities were provided by which worthy students could work out part of the cost. I resolved at once to go to that school. Upon my arrival I was given a job as a janitor, and I was determined to do it so well that no one could find any fault with my job. "

Booker T. Washington said, "No man who continues to add something to the material, intellectual, or moral well-being of the community in which he lives will long be left without proper reward. This is a great human law which cannot be permanently nullified. I believe that any man's life will be filled with constant and unexpected encouragements if he makes up his mind to do his level best each day of his life. That is, he should try to make each day reach as nearly as possible a high-water mark of pure, unselfish and useful living. I pity the man, black or white, who has never experienced the joy and satisfaction that comes to one by reason of an effort to assist in making someone else more useful and more happy. "

Because of the disadvantages at the time of being a minority, he had to work harder and perform his task better in order to secure any recognition. But out of this hard and unusual struggle, through which young Booker was compelled to pass, he got the strength and the self-confidence that one sometimes misses whose pathway is comparatively smooth by reason of his birth, race, or position.

The only name he had ever known was "Booker," but he soon learned that it was the popular thing to have a last name as well as a first. And so when someone asked for his full name, he drew Washington out of the air. The Taliaferro was added later. Here then, was one man who had to do everything for himself, even to choosing his own name.

He had many wonderful experiences at Hampton. He said, "Sometimes I feel that the most valuable lesson I got at the Hampton Institute was in the use and value of the bath. I learned there for the first time some of its value, not only in keeping the body healthy but in inspiring self- respect and promoting virtue." For the first time he slept in a bed that had sheets on it. It was also at Hampton where he got the taste of what it meant to live a life of unselfishness and honor. He told of a man who was seeking a teaching position and was being questioned about his beliefs. One question was concerning the shape of the earth about which there was some controversy. This applicant explained his position in the matter by saying that he was prepared to teach that the earth was either flat or round, according to the preference of the majority of his patrons.

Early in his career he learned the importance of absolute integrity and honor under all circumstances. He said, "My experience has been that the time to test a true gentleman is to observe him when he is in contact with individuals or members of a race that are less fortunate than himself. That is illustrated in no better way than by observing the conduct of a Southern gentleman of the old school when in contact with his former slaves or their descendants."

Booker T. Washington had made such a wonderful, all- around record for good work, integrity, honor, industry, and learning that when he was twenty- three years of age he was recommended to be the head of the proposed new "Negro" school which was about to be established at Tuskegee, Alabama.

When he got to Alabama to begin his new assignment,

there were five boys meeting in an abandoned shack which they had been using as a school house. The five pupils were studying from one book. Two of them were holding the book between them. Behind these two, were two others peeping over the shoulders of the first two, and behind the fourth, was a fifth little fellow who was peeping over the shoulders of all four.

From this beginning in July, 1881, with almost no money except what he himself raised, Booker T. Washington built the great Tuskegee Institute which has done a marvelous work for the African-American race. At Tuskegee, pupils were not only taught from books, but what was even more important, everyone was required to learn to work. The regular school work required three days of actual labor each week. Booker said, "Gradually, by patience and hard work, we brought order out of chaos, just as will be true of any problem if we stick to it with patience, wisdom and earnest effort."

Booker then said, "I learned that assistance given to the weak makes the one who gives it strong, and that oppression to the unfortunate makes one weak. I resolved that I would permit no man, no matter what his color might be, to narrow and degrade my soul by making me hate him."

Booker said, "I have noted time and time again that when an individual perjures himself in dealing with a black man, he soon learns to practice dishonesty in other relationships of life. The white man who begins by cheating a Negro will soon be cheating white men."

Booker T. Washington was too big to be little, too good to be mean. Here was a man of great wisdom. The record of his great success was told in a little book written by himself entitled, *Up from Slavery*. He said, "I have a strong feeling that every individual owes it to himself and to the cause which he is serving to keep a vigorous, healthy body, with the nerves steady and strong, prepared for great efforts and fully prepared for disappointments and trying situations. "

Booker also said, "I make it a rule never to let my work drive me, but to so master it and keep it in such complete control and to keep so far ahead of it that I will be the master instead of the servant. There is a physical, mental and spiritual enjoyment that comes from being the absolute master of one's work in all of its details that is very satisfying and inspiring. My experience teaches me that if one learns to follow this plan, he gets a freshness of body and vigor of mind out of work that goes a long way toward keeping him strong and healthy. I believe that when one can grow to the point where he loves his work, he receives a kind of strength that is invaluable.

"When I begin to work in the morning, I expect to have a successful, pleasant day of it, but at the same time, I prepare for the unpleasant and unexpected that are a part of the life of everyone who expects to accomplish. " He said, "I try to look after the little ills with the idea that if I adequately take care of the little ills, the big ones will largely take care of themselves. "

Booker T. Washington raised himself to great heights and the reasons are easy to see. He became an expert in his human relations. He could always be depended upon. He could be trusted absolutely, in little things or big. He wasted none of his valuable time. He worked hard. He had a burning passion to help his down-trodden people. He became a great orator in their interests.

One of the eastern papers in reporting an address

which he gave in Atlanta at the opening of the Cotton States Exposition in 1895 said:

A Negro Moses stood before a great audience of white people and delivered an oration that marks a new epoch in the history of the South. As he took the platform in that great auditorium, his face was lighted up with the fire of prophecy. It was the first time that any Negro had ever made a speech in the South on any important occasion before an audience composed of white men and women. He electrified the audience, and the response was as if it had come from the throat of a whirlwind. The eyes of the thousands present looked straight at the Negro orator who must rank from this time forth as the foremost man of his race in America.

His voice rang clear and true, and he paused impressively as he made each point. Within ten minutes the multitude was in an uproar of enthusiasm. Handkerchiefs were waved, canes were flourished, hats were tossed in the air. The fairest women of Georgia stood up and cheered. It was as if the orator had bewitched them.

And when he held his dusty hand high above his head, with fingers stretched wide apart and said to the white people of the South on behalf of his race, 'In all things that are human progress, we can be as one as the hand,' a great wave of sound dashed itself against the walls and the whole audience was on its feet in a delirium of applause.

The reporter said, "I have heard the great orators of many countries, but not even Gladstone himself could have pleaded a cause with more consummate power than did this angular Negro, standing in a nimbus of sunshine, surrounded by the very men who had fought to keep his race in bondage. But no matter to what height the roar of applause went, the expression on the face of the orator never changed. Most of the Negroes in the audience were crying, perhaps without knowing just why.

"At the close of the speech, Governor Bullock rushed across the stage and seized the Negro orator's hand. Another shout greeted this demonstration as for a few minutes the two men stood facing each other hand-in-hand. Others came up to congratulate him and some said that this was the first time they had ever called a Negro, 'Mister.'"

Harvard University conferred an honorary degree upon him, the first time such a thing had ever happened to an African-American man. The President of Harvard said, in conferring this honorary degree upon the President of Tuskegee, "Harvard University has honored itself as well as the recipient of this distinction. But," said he, "the degree was not conferred because Mr. Washington is a colored man, or because he was born in slavery, but because he has shown by his work for the elevation of the people of the Black Belt of the South, a genius and a broad humanity that counts for greatness in any man, whether his skin is black or white."

One lecture bureau offered Mr. Washington $50,000 a year, or $200 a night and expenses, if he would place his services at their disposal. To all of these communications he replied that his life's work was at Tuskegee, and that whenever he spoke, it must always be in the interests of the school and of his race. No temptation could compel him even for a moment to lose sight of his mission. He also said, "I have found that the happiest people are those who do the most for others; the most miserable are those who do the least. Say what we will, there is something in human nature which we cannot blot out which makes one man in the end recognize and reward merit in another, regardless of color or race."

Booker T. Washington made his last speech in New Haven on October 25, 1915, an appeal for racial understanding. He was brought back to Tuskegee to die November 14, having given his life in the service of the Tuskegee Institute. His gravestone is a rough-hewn boulder of granite, but his monument is one of the noblest ever created by man—Tuskegee Institute itself.

As a final tribute to him, Elbert Hubbard paraphrased the words of Wendell Philips when he said, "I would call him Napoleon, but Napoleon made his way to empire over broken oaths and through a sea of blood. This man never broke his word. 'No retaliation' is his great motto and the rule of his life. I could call him Cromwell, but Cromwell was only a soldier, and the state he founded went down with him into his grave. I would call him Washington, but the great Virginian, while fighting for freedom, was the owner of slaves.

"But fifty years hence, when Truth gets a hearing, the Muse of History will put Phocion for the Greek, Brutus for the Roman, Hampden for England, Lafayette for France, choose Lincoln as the bright consummate flower of our earlier civilization, and Emerson the ripe fruit of our noonday. Then, dipping her pen in the sunlight, she will write in the clear blue, above them all, the name of the teacher, the orator, the man of affairs—the man of common sense, Booker T.

Washington. "

It is interesting to compare the life of this man who had no opportunities handed him, who had everything against him, who slept on sidewalks, and went without food, yet he rose against great odds from the lowest slavery to the highest pinnacle of American life and accomplishment. While others with every advantage and with every assistance sink by their own weight to failure and oblivion, falling before every obstacle and giving no service. Some have compared this phenomenon with the growth in nature. Nature produces billions of seeds; only a few survive, the weaker perish. It is a part of the law of life. But some unwanted plants have an exuberant growth, while other plants are cultivated carefully, guarded from fungus diseases and insect enemies. Often the uncared for plants are more hardy and successful than the cultivated ones. These plants are often robbed of vitality by coddling.

The lowly plants outside the fence have strength of character. They come up earlier than the tenderly nurtured ones that grow within the enclosure. They may still be flourishing when the short growing span of the latter is finished. You do not have to hoe around them or pick bugs off or spray. They are there because they have already mastered the rules of survival.

GEORGE WASHINGTON

*Unquestioned Devotion
to Duty and Right*

T he ancient Romans had an interesting custom whereby they set up statues of their most illustrious men in their homes. Then, whenever they looked at the images before them, they thought about the qualities of the great men they represented, and thus they themselves were lifted up. In America we do something very similar. We set aside holidays to commemorate the birthdays of our greatest men. We underline their virtues and talk about the qualities that made each of them great. On each February 22, we center our appreciation and admiration on the Father of our country, George Washington. We not only erected statues to the memory of Washington, but our national capitol was also named in his honor.

In 1844, a white marble obelisk was erected as a national memorial in Washington, D. C. This giant marble shaft, 55 feet square at its base, reaches 555 feet into the sky. It is one of the loftiest and most imposing monuments ever reared by man. It is taller than the pyramids. It reaches far above the cathedral domes of St. Paul's or St. Peter's.

An actual image of Washington could only display him in one phase of his varied character. But this lofty marble shaft fitly typifies the upward reaches of his exalted life. It also serves as a symbol of our national greatness and destiny.

One of Washington's greatest admirers and most enthusiastic followers was Abraham Lincoln. Washington died ten years before Lincoln was born, yet he probably did more to shape Lincoln's character and aim in life than any other man who ever lived.

Lincoln said, "Washington is the mightiest name on earth, long since mightiest in the cause of civil liberty, still mightiest in moral reformation. On that name a eulogy is expected that cannot be. To add brightness to the sun or glory to the name of Washington is alike impossible. Let none attempt it. In solemn awe pronounce the name and in its naked deathless splendor, leave it shining on. "

What Washington did for Lincoln, he could do for us if we properly practice the process of transferring virtues. The greatness of Washington continues to shine upon us, undiminished by any passage of time. Shortly after Washington's death, General Henry Lee referred to him on the floor of the House of Representatives as, "the man first in war, first in peace, and first in the hearts of his countrymen. "

Washington was born February 22, 1732. His father died before George was 12 years old. George had little formal schooling, but he had enough good common sense to lift him to the level of genius. He soon learned to bear responsibility well and to meet difficulty courageously. Washington joined the army but refused to accept any pay for his services. He learned as he fought, eliminating his early errors as he gained experience. His devotion to his country was without flaw. He thoroughly mastered his profession, and emerged from the war without a peer.

George stood six and a half feet tall. He was of fine physical form, the finest horseman, and the knightliest figure of his time. He seemed designed by nature to lead, and he was always ready when bold strokes were required and the outcome of the battle was reposed in a single man. There are always critical moments in a campaign when if the mind hesitates or the nerve flinches, all may be lost. But Washington was always equal to every occasion.

As we look up to his marble shaft, a panorama of his life may pass before us. Mr. John Warwick Daniel has said in substance, we go with him as he crosses the Delaware on that black December night to attack the enemy at Trenton. The shrieking winds and up heaving of great blocks of ice in the river would have petrified a leader of less hardy mold.

We behold him at Monmouth while he is turning back his own retreating lines. He rode his white charger along the ranks until his horse was shot out from under him. Then, leaping upon his Arabian bay, he continued shouting encouragement to his men. After observing his feats of courage and deeds of honor, Lafayette exclaimed, "Never did I behold so superb a man."

We see him again at Princeton, dashing through a storm of lead to rally his wavering troops. He bolts into the thickest of the fray. Colonel Fitzgerald, his aide, reined his own horse, and pulled his hat down over his eyes that he might not see his chieftain fall. Then, through the smoke, Washington reappears, waving his hat, cheering on his men and shouting, "Bring up the troops for the day is ours."

Mr. Daniel says, "Even Richard the Lion Hearted

might well have doffed his plume to such a chief. As a great knight he met his foe full tilt, and in the shock of battle hurled one after another to the ground. "

Washington kept together a starved, unpaid, and suffering army by his personal firmness, patience, and judicious handling of men. In the midst of blank despair, neither his heart nor his purpose wavered. He defeated the best-trained generals of Europe. And yet, as we look back on those revolutionary years, we see clearly that the greatest factor in the final success was not his military greatness; it was the confidence inspired by Washington the man, rather than his great genius as a soldier. His character made him the only man who could have carried the Revolution to a successful conclusion.

As a statesman, Washington shined at his best. He had a more infallible discrimination of circumstances and men than any of his contemporaries. He weighed his facts in a more just scale. He walked the dizzy heights of power in the perfect balance of every faculty.

Washington lived by the principles of the Declaration of Independence, that "to secure the inalienable rights of man, governments were instituted amongst men deriving their just powers from the consent of the governed; and that whenever any form of government becomes destructive of these ends, it is the right of the people to alter or abolish it, and to institute a new government, laying its foundation on such principles and organizing its powers in such forms as to them shall seem most likely to affect their safety and happiness. "

If we seek an explanation of the greatness of Washington himself, it will not be found in his unusual mind, for Franklin's mind was greater. Neither will it be found in his energy nor ingenuity, for Benedict Arnold surpassed him in these qualities. It will not be in his military experience, for Charles Lee's was far more extensive. The secret of Washington's success lay in the strength of his character. Day by day, his absolute fairness and unquestioned devotion to duty and right won the love of his soldiers and the perfect confidence of his countrymen.

Character is the rarest manifestation of genius, and it demands more constructive faculties and even a higher kind of heroism than that exhibited in actual battle. Washington won the independence of the American states, not so much by what he *knew* or even by what he *did*, but because of what he *was*. He was divinely inspired to point out the path that American destiny should follow. He brought to pass great things as the Father of his country.

Although he was invested with the powers of a dictator, yet his country felt not the slightest distrust of his integrity. He had none of the blemishes so common in the tyrants of our day, and "as history has lifted the visor of his helmet, it has disclosed the visage of a sage. "

But Washington's service to his country did not end with his final military victory. As he had been the greatest in war, he was also the most fit to lead his country in peace. At the end of the war the army was disbanded and the soldiers went back to their homes. When Washington was released, the danger of possible anarchy became seriously apparent. "America, poor, exhausted, weeping and bleeding, lay agonizing upon her bed of laurels. " When the military effort was replaced, the states began to go their separate ways. Washington was the only source of authority that had more than a local influence. Without him, the Union might well have lost its cohesion, and the nation that we know might have died before it was born by degenerating into a number of independent hostile states.

To many there seemed but one escape from the storm that threatened, and that was to make Washington king. In the army, this plan was very seriously considered; but when it was mentioned to Washington, he was pained that such an idea should ever exist. He said, "I am at a loss to conceive what part of my conduct could have given encouragement to such an idea, fraught as it is with the greatest mischief that could befall our country. " He said, "Let me conjure you, if you have any regard for your country, yourselves, or your posterity, or if you have any respect for me, banish these thoughts immediately from your mind. " How strange that sounds in our day of power- mad dictators!

Although without civil authority in this period between war and peace, yet it was here that Washington rose to his highest stature, impelled by this natural impulse in his soul that would not allow him to see the hopes of a nation perish. He addressed a circular to all of the people in which he said, "Convinced of the importance of this crisis, silence in me would be a crime. " The foundations of our whole national structure trembled, having no cement except Washington to hold its stones together.

Mr. Daniel further said of Washington, "Soldier, patriot, statesman, sage, reformer of creeds, teacher of truth and justice, achiever and preserver of liberty, the first of men, founder and savior of his country, and the Father of his people. This is he, solitary and unapproachable in his grandeur. " He said, "O felicitous providence that gave to America our Washington. "

When the delegates of the Constitutional Convention

assembled at Philadelphia, Washington would listen to no half-way measures. He said, "Let us raise a standard to which the wise and the just can repair." When the work of the convention began, he was chosen as its president. Under his leadership came the great American Constitution, which Gladstone, the British Prime Minister, declared to be the greatest document ever struck off by the hand of man.

Washington was sworn in as the first President of the United States on April 30, 1789. What a noble figure to stand in the forefront of a nation's history and give it its start toward its destiny. His simple, honest manner was well suited for the beginning of a great republic, and his own self-mastery was a lasting lesson to democracy.

After eight years of holding the reigns of national power, Washington refused re-election and bid farewell to the people he had served through a generation. Tears coursed down his cheeks as he turned for the last time from those he had counseled in both war and peace, love and sorrow. Three years after his retirement from public life, as he lay dying, he felt his own waning pulse and murmured, "It is well."

It has been said of Washington, "He had drawn his sword from patriotic impulse without ambition and without malice. He had wielded it without vindictiveness, and he had sheathed it without reproach. Keeping faith in all things, he left us bewildered with the splendid problem of whether to admire him most for what he was, or for what he would never consent to be, as over and above all of his virtues was the matchless manhood of his personal honor on which temptation dared not smile or on which suspicion never once cast a frown."

Though George Washington is dead, his spirit will live on forever. On the anniversary of his birth, we might well look up to the monumental symbolic shaft and repledge ourselves to the divinely-inspired principles for which he stood, that this nation, under God, shall go on to its destiny. George Byron paid this tribute to George Washington:

> Where may the wearied eye repose
> When gazing on the great
> Where neither guilty glory grows
> Nor despicable state.
> Yes one, the first—the last—the best
> That Cincinnatus of the West
> Whom envy dared not date,
> Bequeathed the name of Washington
> To make men blush, there was but one.

Long live the memory and ideals of this great man. May the America that he established always remain the citadel of Liberty. As we look up again and again to the marble shaft symbolizing his life and the great nation that he founded, we might well commit ourselves as did the founding fathers, saying, "In the support of his declaration, we mutually pledge to each other our lives, our fortunes, and our sacred honor."

STERLING W. SILL

A Lover of Books,
A Seeker of Truth,
A Believer in Greatness

The only person unanimously selected to be honored in the *Hall of Fame for Great Americans* was George Washington. The last person honored was Franklin D. Roosevelt in 1976. After visiting this awe-inspiring memorial to success, located in New York, I more fully understood the admonition given by Sterling W. Sill when he said, "Build your own private sanctuary reserved exclusively for those great men and women who can most profitably influence the direction and extent of your life and who are most able to set your heart afire with devotion to truth." It is with humble admiration that I have selected this very man to be a part of my personal hall of fame. Sterling W. Sill sought knowledge at the feet of the noblest and greatest minds in history and lived a life so closely resembling theirs that he influenced millions of people to reach for, and obtain, that same greatness.

Case number 4345 on the books of the Carnegie Hero Foundation describes the dramatic rescue of a thirteen-year old boy, George Redding, from drowning in the Atlantic

Ocean on January 21, 1959. George had been swimming with a family friend, and although they were quite far from shore, a sandbar supported their feet allowing them to enjoy the surf. The lighthearted fun faded quickly as George became separated from his friend by the swift tide. The depth of the water and the force of the waves increased dramatically causing fear and panic. Calling out for help, George exhibited the classic signs of drowning. His 56-year old companion acted quickly.

It has been said that responsibilities gravitate to the person who can shoulder them. George narrowly escaped death because a man, who embodied the most admirable characteristics of some of the greatest heroes in history, called upon a deep reservoir of strength to win this child's life. Sterling W. Sill understood responsibility and was the recipient of the awesome power that comes from living a life of study, of learning, and of focus on principles that build strong men and women. It was not with his hands alone that he reached for George as the ocean current exerted its force against both of their lives. The strength, the determination, the faith, and the courage of such giants as Napoleon the Great, Abraham Lincoln, the Prophet Job, and Joan of Arc powered his muscles as he refused to give up something so sacred as the life of this young boy.

George was the son of a friend and business associate to Sterling W. Sill who had accompanied his father on a five-day business convention in Florida. Sill worked for New York Life Insurance Company and had, by the time of this event, risen to a place of prestige in the insurance field for his record breaking sales teams and enthusiastic work ethic. George was fortunate to have as his companion that day a man who exemplified the words of Tennyson, "I am a part of all that I have met. " Sill had devoted every spare moment in his life to meeting the great heroes of the past through what he called the majesty of books. "I imagine this shelf in my library to contain a great collection of human beings where I may have the better of each one as his service is needed. The contribution of each may be brief in itself, but whatever may have been possessed of inspiration, dedication, and righteousness now belongs to me. How else but in a book can one go back into the past for a visit in ancient Rome or Gethsemane or Gettysburg? How else can we share in the wealth of the great thinkers who bring about the progress of the world? Books may contain the distilled essence of the greatest lives. They abound in inspiration and provide a motivation for the most magnificent accomplishment. "

On January 21, 1959, Sterling W. Sill became a hero. The decision to leave the safety of the sand bar and risk his own life to reach for the drowning boy was made without hesitation. As Sill attempted the rescue, George became gripped with panic and pulled both of them under the water. Struggling to keep himself from drowning as well, Sill was able to position George on his back and head for the safety of the nearby sandbar. Believing this was better than trying to make it all the way back to shore, he headed parallel to it. The sandbar did not appear and Sill began to lose strength and swallow water.

Most men and women would have begun to weigh their own chances of survival at this point. Realizing that the rescue could fail and result in the loss of two lives, the desire to let go and save oneself would be overwhelming. Fortunately for George, Sterling had trained his mind to think in a manner that did not accept defeat. He believed that the greatest invention ever perfected, even by God himself, was the human mind.

If we can learn to operate it successfully, it can make us rich in every resource. The key to success in all aspects of our lives is our own thoughts. What we are, and what we will become, will be determined by what and how we think. Sterling W. Sill was a master at his craft, and in all his works spoke of the great men and women he had studied. He lived by the creed that knowledge illuminates the path, action powers the engine, and that character mans the controls. With this conviction embedded in his soul, Sill made four more attempts to find the sandbar, and with each attempt swallowed more and more water into his lungs. In his words describing the final moments, we get a glimpse of what it means to be a hero.

> Then I took a last look at the shore which seemed to be way off in the distance. I had no sensation of choking or suffocating. It was as though I were floating around on a soft comfortable cloud. The only unpleasant sensation I had was my feeling against myself for causing my own death as well as that of my good friend, George, when neither of us were ready for that event to take place. Just before I lost all strength, I heard a voice and I knew that someone was speaking to me. And his face was probably within a foot and half of my own, and yet I could not see him. I did not recognize his voice, nor could I understand even one word of what he said. But, I felt the boy's grip relax around my throat and I knew that someone was taking him off my back. Then I thought maybe I could swim.

That someone was Robert E. Mitchell, Jr. who had

been snorkeling nearby and brought George safely to the shore. Sill was unable to save himself as the current took him further out to sea and water filled his lungs. Calling out for help, followed by a loss of consciousness, he remembers only the sensation of drowning. Robert, returning to the water, then saved the life of Sterling W. Sill.

The rescue of this young boy was just one of the many legendary aspects of Sill's life. Focus and diligence was applied in all areas of his life and the richness he was granted as a result was then shared with millions of people through books, speeches, seminars and radio broadcasts. Sill spoke of his passion for learning and his strong conviction that as Napoleon stated when asked about the conditions of Rome, "I make conditions!" Indeed, thoughts do rule the world.

Sill believed that all of our thoughts do not have to be original ones. Instead, we can become acquainted with and memorize the greatest ideas of others until these ideas become as much a part of us as if we had been the first to think of them. "The constructive ideas, uplifting philosophies, and great scriptural passages that we memorize make up our mental substance just as bricks make up the substance of a wall. And if we become effective in this important construction process, we can build our lives to any desired specification." We can think and grow rich, we can think and grow faithful, and we can think and grow better.

The Apostle Paul teaches in Romans 12:2, ". . . be ye transformed by the renewing of your mind." Sterling W. Sill's transformation began in 1942 during WWII when he attended a lecture on the value of great literature. The speaker posed this question to the audience, "If you were going to be a prisoner in a concentration camp for the next four years and could take with you the works of any ten authors, which would you take?" He suggested that each person select ten authors that they would most like to resemble and then exhaust each one in turn by reading everything the author had ever written. He then listed his own selections. Not only did Sill read all ten of those books, he also marked the passages that appealed to him and memorized them as he walked to and from work. One of the great paradoxes of life is that almost everyone wants to improve his circumstances, but to improve one's self takes a diligent and concentrated man. Sterling W. Sill would go on to read more than a thousand of the world's most treasured books. He said,

> I decided to read every word that Shakespeare wrote. That is, I decided to rethink every idea that Shakespeare ever thought, to run through my brain every idea that ever went through his brain . . . I had a pretty hard time . . . I had to re-read . . . I had a tremendous experience with Shakespeare as I read his great speeches, felt the power of his motivation, and watched the players upon his stage as they acted and reacted upon each other.
>
> After Shakespeare, I read 987 of the great classics that have stood the test of time, and I have all of the potent passages and other great ideas all catalogued in my notebooks, a substantial part of which I have memorized.
>
> Then in turn I read the works of Emerson who has been called the greatest thinker that America had ever produced. And I would like to have some of his ideas made negotiable in my own bloodstream.

I also read twenty-eight volumes of Elbert Hubbard including the 14 volumes of *Little Journeys into the Lives of Great Men* wherein I found qualities of some of the greatest who have ever lived and I desired to have those same qualities. What we love and desire and work for will come to us, this law of attraction never fails.

And then I read the fifty volumes of the Harvard Classics. Many years ago President Charles W. Eliot of Harvard got some of his finest scholars together to compile the greatest ideas that had ever been thought or spoken in the world into one set of volumes called the Harvard Classics; I can go through them now and make myself the beneficiary of many lifetimes of work . . . I always read with my pen. I mark only those ideas that do something for me.

Sill was known for always reading with his pen in hand ready to enhance his paper memory. He clearly embodied the wisdom of Emerson to clean out all discords. He believed that if you are always engaged in focused thought upon the ideas and the lessons spoken of by Socrates, the Apostle Paul, Joan of Arc, or Emerson, your mind will start responding as their minds did. Choosing the lessons from such great lives requires diligent effort; however, the reward is beyond measure. Great lives have left a pattern to be duplicated for our own effectiveness, for our success, for our own richness. Sill used the following method to reap the greatest reward. "I think of my reading in terms of a combined harvester out on the farm. It sweeps across a field of wheat and cuts everything before it. Then it operates a threshing process by which it throws out all the weeds, the chaff, and the straw, and puts the clean wheat into the sack. I do a similar kind of mental threshing. I mark all of the ideas that I think will be helpful to me. Then I make some decisions about them and prepare myself to utilize them in my own life. These especially selected ideas now fill twenty-five notebooks totaling some 7,500 pages. Then I have gone back and reviewed and memorized the most interesting and exciting of these ideas. The rest I stamp as deeply as possible into my brain cells so that I have an intimate speaking acquaintanceship with those I have not memorized." Sterling W. Sill read the books and he became the man, a richer man in all areas of his life.

Surprisingly, Sill also read literature that was contrary to what he believed as far as the existence of God. "I have never had any serious opposition to my faith, and I wondered what would have happened if I had been exposed to some serious anti-religion. And so I read 19,900 pages from the man who, in my opinion, was the greatest atheist in the world. Robert G. Ingersoll was an orator, a salesman, a persuader; and I thought that if anybody could change my faith, it might be him. And so I read, so far as I know, every one of his ideas on atheism, which would be the equivalent in volume of some eighty new testaments, and I felt not the slightest problem so far as my faith was concerned. That is, my faith was not shaken in the slightest degree."

A *builder of men* is the accolade given to Sterling W. Sill by his business associates. Mr. B. Woodbury, the Vice-President of Zion's National Bank, stated, "I don't know of any person in this country who has a record of recruiting and motivating men equal to that which Sill enjoys." His awards were staggering, and the growth of the company under his leadership was monumental.

Sill was described by fellow workers as a hard taskmaster, who expected more than marginal effort, and wanted people to love their work as he did. As a man of action, who took only six days off from work during a twenty-nine year period, he believed that the passion he held for his work was his vacation. "What a thrilling experience life offers each one of us as we take hold of our share of the work of the world and minister to the needs of our fellow men that we may learn to do it with excellence and honor, that we may build these contour lines of our lives to put ourselves in the purer air that goes with honorable labor and effective accomplishment. "

This work ethic proved to have a powerful effect in the lives of those whom Sill mentored and associated with. Housed in the J. Willard Marriott Library at the University of Utah, are thirty-four boxes containing thousands of letters of gratitude and praise sent to Sterling W. Sill. People from all walks of life, including CEO's of numerous companies, presidents and leaders of various universities, life insurance agents, and just ordinary listeners of his radio addresses and speeches, felt compelled to thank him for the richness they gained by living the principles he taught and exemplified.

Work is not just the way we get our bread; it is how we build our character, develop our personality, learn initiative, cause our bodies to grow, and do almost every other worthwhile thing in the world. For twenty-five years, while at New York Life, Sill helped build better people that would in turn, build a better company by teaching and motivating them through a weekly training bulletin that he prepared. "I tried to persuade these agents that if they would take at least one good sales idea each week and thoroughly master it by memorization and practice, it would not be very long before their skills would be greatly increased and available to help them to push themselves a little higher up the ladder of accomplishment. That is, sales knowledge must be available not only in his sales brain, but sales skills must also be available in his sales muscles. " This weekly bulletin became so widely sought after that agents and managers from across the country were requesting it by the thousands. One such publication of Sill's, entitled "Selecting Your Life's Work, " was distributed to 750,000 New York Life agents and prospective agents.

Sill's advice on becoming better at one's vocation was quite simple. Be a better person and store up as much knowledge as you possibly can. No matter what field of work is chosen, an "idea bank" will yield tremendous revenues. Sill explained, "When in my reading I come to some little nugget of an idea that sends a chill up and down my backbone and gives me ambition to do something important, I take that out and put it in my idea bank, and then when I have time I memorize it. One of the reasons why we have banks to put our money in is to keep it from slipping through our fingers. The pocket is not a very suitable place to keep valuable possessions, nor is the head a very good place to keep ideas. In the first place, the brain was never intended as a warehouse; it is a workroom. The brain does not serve very well as an idea bank because it is so full of leaks. A good way to avoid losing ideas is to write them down while they are fresh. Great men have always been bankers of ideas. Robert Louis Stevenson always carried with him two books: one to read from and one to write in. "

You may judge a man more truly by the books and the papers that he reads than by the social companions which he keeps. This was the belief of Sterling W. Sill along with the principle that "a regular period of study set aside each day over a few years could make each of us a genius in living. It could make us the beneficiaries of all the great and good who have ever lived. Reading is the process by which we take possession of this fabulous inheritance. It enables us to live a thousand lives in one. " Sill blended the character of all the great lives he had studied into his very being. At the age of seventy-two, after a life of amazing accomplishment, he still had a great hunger for study. Just as we frequently need an appraisal on our home for a refinance or a listing before selling, Sill knew that our lives needed appraisal constantly. George Washington Carver, famous for his agricultural and humanitarian contributions to the world, stated, "Every human being has an obligation to leave the soil richer than when he found it. "

Sterling W. Sill may have been the most influential man the world never knew. In his words, he gave this counsel, "I believe in everlasting life, in everlasting progress, and in everlasting happiness. Henry David Thoreau once said, 'I am afraid that at the last I may discover when it is too late, that I have missed the joy. ' We need to know the joy of being alive, the joys of excellence, and the joys of truth. We need to know the joys of labor, the joys of family, and the joys of being genuine. It is wonderful to make a profit, it is great to develop prominence, it is stimulating to acquire fame; but even glory has no halo if we miss the joy. During my many years I have loved life, I have been broadened by the law, I have been inspired by love, I have been thrilled by success, and I have gloried in struggle and hardship. But I thank the great God of the universe that I have not missed the joy. " Lessons such as this, if studied and learned, will provide a richness and abundance in life that can be obtained in no other way.

CONCLUSION

I trust that the columns of this book are now filled with your new ideas of how great lives can move you to action! An attitude of, "If it's going to be... it's up to me," should permeate your mind. This book should not be a casual read for the desiring soul. Instead, it should be an infusion of possibilities and enthusiasm of what you can accomplish. The great philosopher, Socrates, was speaking to each of us when he said,

> I do nothing but go about persuading you all, old and young alike, not to take thought for your persons or your properties, but and chiefly, to care about the greatest improvement of the soul. I tell you that virtue is not given by money, but that from virtue comes money and every other good of man, public as well as private.

Short cuts to success are being flaunted by self-proclaimed experts at every turn, but few, if any, actually get you to your desired destination. Leonardo da Vinci incorporated in his life's work the principle of *saper vedere* which means knowing how to see, or broadening your view by studying the work of others. He craved knowledge that would illuminate the possibilities of his creativity and of his talents. Create your own personal Hall of Fame; place people in it that will inspire your upward reach. Develop the habits, skills, and attitudes that are an embodiment of these extraordinary people you just read about and you will become rich in all areas of your life.

Take action now to infuse your life with possibilities. Go to *www.LessonsfromGreatLives.com* to vote on your favorite life and write about what has inspired you.

Oliver Wendell Homes has said, "A mind once stretched to a new idea never returns to its original dimensions."

Bibliography

Hubbard, Elbert. _Selected Writings_. Vol. 10. East Aurora, NY:
Roy Crofters, 1928.

Sill, Sterling W. _Bottles and Books_. Brigham Young University,
Provo, UT. 1 May 1977.

Sill, Sterling W. _How to Personally Profit from the Laws of Success_.
Salt Lake City, UT: National Institute of Financial
Planning, Inc, 1984.

Sill, Sterling W. _Lessons from Great Lives_. Bountiful, UT:
Horizon Publishers & Distributors, 1981.

Sill, Sterling W. _The Best of Sterling W. Sill_. Salt Lake City, UT:
Bookcraft, Inc, 1983.

Sill, Sterling W. _The Laws of Success_. Salt Lake City, UT:
Deseret Book Company, 1975.

Sill, Sterling W. _The Majesty of Books_. Salt Lake City, UT:
Deseret Book Company, 1974.

Sill, Sterling W. _The Miracle of Personality_. Salt Lake City, UT:
Bookcraft, Inc, 1966.

Sill, Sterling W. _The Nine Lives of Sterling W. Sill_. Bountiful, UT:
Horizons Publishers & Distributors, 1979.

Sill, Sterling W. *The Power of Believing*. Salt Lake City, UT:
          Bookcraft, Inc. 1968.

Sill, Sterling W. *The Three Infinities*. Salt Lake City, UT:
          Bookcraft, Inc, 1969.

Sill, Sterling W. *The Way of Success*. Salt Lake City, UT:
          Bookcraft, Inc, 1964.

About the Authors

Sterling W. Sill

A prolific author of over 30 books on personal development, training and motivation, Sterling W. Sill rose to great heights of success as an agent for New York Life Insurance Company. For the better part of forty years, he consistently set sales records and achieved the highest lifetime recruiting statistics in the entire company. Sill was unequaled as a recruiter, trainer, and motivator, but most importantly, he was admired and loved by all of his associates. For seventeen years he spoke on a weekly radio program that was carried by 370 stations. He taught principles of success gleaned from reading more than a thousand of the world's most treasured books. Reading, he said, allows us to profit from any great man's life without its risk. As a successful business man, civic and church leader, educator, speaker and writer, Sill embodied admirable characteristics of the greatest who ever lived. As a result, he touched the lives of everyone he met.

Dan McCormick

In 1984 at the age of 22, Dan McCormick and his wife, Marilyn, earned their first million dollars through direct sales. Since that time, Dan has propelled his career forward at top speed, surpassing even his own expectations. His unbridled enthusiasm and adrenaline pumping interaction with everyone he meets often raises the question, "How does he do it?" As a sought after speaker and enormously successful distributor with Nu Skin Enterprises, Dan has achieved success not by a formal education, but instead, through a focused and persistent study of great men and women whom he refers to as "the oracles of human development." Having earned millions of dollars by building his business that includes tens of thousands of distributors world-wide, Dan McCormick is a man worth listening to.

Acknowledgements

The city of Alexandria, Egypt has quite a history! Founded by Alexander the Great in 332 B. C. as the Greek capital of Egypt, it soon became the hub for commerce and learning. The Royal Library of Alexandria was once the largest library in the world. A majority of the manuscripts that were held in this vast storehouse of ancient wisdom were destroyed by fire and because they had been handwritten, the writings were impossible to replace.

The technology of today allows us to access our modern repositories of knowledge with the click of a button. This concept would be astounding to the great philosophers, scientists and poets who lived in ancient times. While books written hundreds of years ago were rare, expensive and difficult to come by, today they can be bought for just a few dollars. We are indeed fortunate to have this luxury at our fingertips.

For some time, I have had a love affair with books. Any inspiration or writings that could assist me in becoming more informed as to how to live a better life, I was interested in absorbing. To be grateful for every author I have ever read and life ever lived that added to my experience is a pleasurable thing. It has now come time for me to express gratitude to the many people who have contributed to the fulfillment of my quest to reprint, rejuvenate, and make necessary additions to this masterful work by Sterling W. Sill.

To Kristina Booth, my co-writer, editor, and assistant for research, organization, and composition, I express my sincerest gratitude. Her passion for learning and her precise attention to detail contributed to this work immensely. She shared my enthusiasm, she gave structure to my thoughts, and most of all, she encouraged the pursuit of my dream to change lives for the better.

I will always be in awe of the artistic talent of Bill Suman, of William Suman Design, Inc. His creativity produced this impressive book cover and page design. Bill knows how to make magic happen in print!

A special thanks to William Werfelman, at New York Life Insurance Company for his gracious support in providing materials and historical documents pertaining to the amazing man, Sterling W Sill. I also want to express my gratitude to the University of Utah and the J. Willard Marriot Library for the wealth of information they provided.

My appreciation is also extended to Art and Susan Zuckerman, Directors of The Hall of Fame for Great Americans, Deseret Book Company, and Brigham Young University for rights granted.

To the following people who aided my research or provided inspiration and support, I offer my thanks: Kevin Hall, Dave Blanchard, Richard Paul Evans, Cynthia Kersey, Troy Dunn, TJ Hoisington, Diane Bauer, Lon Wardrop, Crystal McCormick, and Sterling G. Sill.

It has been said, "When you're on a journey, and the end keeps getting further and further away, then you realize that the real end is the journey." To all who have traveled with me, I acknowledge your contribution and extend my sincerest gratitude.

Share *Lessons from Great Lives* with your Friends, Family, and Colleagues

(Audio Book & Quantity Discounts Available)

SHARE WITH US

· VOTE for your favorite Great Life.
· SUBMIT a story of a great life that has impacted yours.
· READ and comment on the blog.

WE WANT TO INSPIRE YOUR ORGANIZATION

Do you have an audience that could benefit from Dan McCormick's extraordinary presentation on illuminating the path to success in all areas of our lives?

Focusing on the great men and women who have paved the way for us to follow, Dan dispels the myths and focuses on time tested wisdom from the oracles of human development.

To arrange a speaking engagement with Dan McCormick visit:

www.LessonsfromGreatLives.com

NOTES

NOTES

AYLESBURY
PUBLISHING